Pla

Le

Spaces

Planning
Learning
Spaces

**A PRACTICAL GUIDE FOR ARCHITECTS,
DESIGNERS AND SCHOOL LEADERS**

Murray Hudson and Terry White

Forewords by Herman Hertzberger
and Sir Ken Robinson

CONTRIBUTORS
Professor Peter Barrett, Alastair Blyth,
Rosan Bosch, Professor Andrew Brewerton,
James Clarke, Mark Clarke, Peter Clegg,
Michál Cohen, Shane Cryer, Delphine Dryer,
Robin Dryer, Lene Jensby Lange, Richard
Leonard, Andy Piggott, Diane Pumphrey,
Kerri Ranney, Gary Spracklen, Dave Strudwick,
Joe Jack Williams

LAURENCE KING PUBLISHING

CONTENTS

Opposite
Planning spaces for us

A new approach for now

Look around: global education is in a state of flux. Governments are urgently trying to educate the next generation for jobs that do not yet exist

Others understand that their future depends upon a workforce that is educated for an evolving world, and is able to adapt to ongoing change. What and how we teach are being hotly debated within countries and between continents. But do we talk enough about *where* we teach? Possibly not, but we should do.

Recent academic research has shown that the physical space in which children are taught has a direct impact on learning outcomes. In the UK, the recent Holistic Evidence and Design (HEAD) study, looking at 3,766 children in 137 classrooms from 27 very different primary schools, found that the physical characteristics of classrooms accounted for a 16 per cent variation in children's learning capabilities. This is significant and proves conclusively that the learning environment does matter.

Visionary educationalist Loris Malaguzzi famously described the classroom as the 'third teacher', next to pupils and teachers themselves. We have gathered evidence from around the world that establishes links between the design of the spaces in which young people learn and better learning outcomes.

Architects have much to consider when approaching a new school project: there are competing agendas – from politicians to parents; teaching methods are constantly evolving; technology is invading the classroom and other learning spaces; and there are financial implications to every decision.

In this book we address the big questions surrounding the twenty-first century educational agenda and the learning spaces and buildings required to support it. To do this, we have assembled some of the finest educational leaders and innovative school architects to share their hard-earned wisdom. We have input from across the world – from Europe, the Gulf States, the USA and Australasia. We address the various issues that impact the design of school buildings.

We will show you how to get the basics – fresh air, light, heat and acoustics – right, while also considering sustainability. We reveal how to create a sense of belonging and engagement for all students, and provide an understanding of how furniture and technology interact with space. And we also address the intangibles of how schools must nurture the creativity present in all of us.

The advice contained is no-nonsense and practical. It does, however, require your thinking and engagement to determine the learning approaches and teaching practices that are fit for the twenty-first century. It is up to you to translate the advice into the design of exciting new projects. You can create inspiring learning spaces that empower the next student generation. Here's how.

Murray Hudson and Terry White

Opposite
A learning stairway.
Stephen Perse Foundation
School, Cambridge, UK

Rethinking school design

Designing schools may not be professionally glamorous, but the result has the greatest impact on our lives

Our characters as adults are rooted in the experiences we have as children, influenced in particular by our early built surroundings. As a child you need to be content both at home and at school in order to reach your potential. So, the onus is on architects, educators and parents to try to provide the best environments for children to develop both intellectually and emotionally. The design of schools is one of the most important areas of architecture, because it can have one of the greatest impacts on shaping lives. Yet, as an area of architectural practice, it has never received the attention it deserves. Maybe this is because it is not seen as professionally glamorous. This publication, however, like my own books over the years, seeks to correct this and to inspire the design of more intelligent learning spaces.

There are essentially two ways of educating people: one way is to tell them how the world works – a sort of 'this is how it is… so remember!'; the other way is to let people develop a capacity for thinking for themselves. I was lucky enough to have been educated at a time when there was the belief that children should be allowed to develop their own spirit. Today, I fear education is tending towards the opposite, and there's a return to an 'old school' style of teaching. As an architect who has spent his whole career designing schools, when I enter a learning space I can see at a glance what the pedagogical ethos of the place is just by looking at the layout of the classrooms.

The goal should be to create spaces that provide the best possible learning environment, where a child can feel safe, emotionally connected and intellectually stimulated. When I'm designing a school, it is always related to what people will do with it, what people will think of it. For me, form, space and people are absolutely complementary. I can't think of designing any another way. Fundamentally, successful school design is all about creating 'unofficial' spaces, which are not functionally defined but can be interpreted and owned by the people who use them. This means designing spaces that are adaptive, so that they can embrace inevitable change. One also needs to design the overall space so that areas intended for individual activity are in functional harmony with larger ones that bring people together.

Over the years, I have introduced features into schools that enhance navigation and create that all-important sense of place, such as islands, pits or grandstands. They provide orientation and domestication, both of which provoke feelings of familiarity and connection. This sense of attachment in turn enables children to take emotional ownership of a space, so it becomes their own place. In the end, the design of schools should centre on creating the feeling of homecoming. But more than this, you are also trying to give a child not only the feeling of home, safety and comfort, but also the desire and confidence to seek out new horizons, experiences and adventures.

I know from over 60 years of practice that the thoughtful planning of learning spaces can achieve these kinds of life-determining results.

Herman Hertzberger

Building creativity into school design

Across the globe, there is a growing movement to transform education to help students to meet the real challenges of living and learning in the twenty-first century. Transforming education means reimagining schools

There are important differences between learning, education and school. Learning is acquiring new knowledge and skills; education is a planned programme of learning; a school is a community where education is meant to happen. Children love to learn; however, they don't always enjoy education, and some have serious problems with school. Those problems are often to do with the culture of schools, including the physical spaces they inhabit.

What is a school? A school is a community of learners: a group of people who come together to learn with and from each other. By 'culture' I mean a community's overall way of life. In schools as in other organized communities, culture includes *habits* and *habitats*. Habits are a community's characteristic forms of behaviour, and the values and purposes that underpin them; habitat is the physical environment the community occupies. In designed spaces, the habitat is meant to facilitate a community's habits, at least in theory. In practice, there is a constant osmosis between them. As Winston Churchill famously put it, 'We shape our buildings: thereafter they shape us.' Consequently, changing the culture of education also involves rethinking the spaces in which it happens.

Since the spread of mass education from the nineteenth century, schools have evolved into certain sorts of institutions with typical habits and habitats. Conventionally, children are educated by age groups in different types of schools, each with different sorts of 'age-appropriate' cultures. Typically, in the early years, children sit in circles and do practical things in groups; in later years they sit down, face the front and take notes. By then, the curriculum is often divided into hierarchies of separate subjects according to their supposed utility, and the day into specific units of time marked out by bells and transitions, for organizational efficiency. School buildings have been designed accordingly with separate classrooms and facilities to support these practices, which they then reinforce. Not all schools are like this and schools do not *need* to be like this at all. For a host of reasons, it is increasingly important that they are not.

In recent years, education has become a hot political issue – mainly for economic reasons – and the drive to raise standards has led to more standardization, specialization, testing, and competition between students, teachers, schools and even countries. For the most part, these strategies are not working, for

teachers, students or their families, and there is a pressing movement for change: a movement towards forms of education that facilitate curiosity, creativity, collaboration and a genuine love of learning. This movement recognizes that from the moment they are born, children are driven by a deep curiosity to explore the world around them. Compulsory education occupies the most formative years of their lives. From birth to adolescence, if the conditions are right, they undergo a dramatic metamorphosis: they develop physically, socially, cognitively, emotionally and spiritually. A balanced, dynamic education and great schools should provide equally for all of these.

The task of good school design is to create the best physical environment – the best habitat – for that to happen. For that reason, reimagining schools is one of the most creative challenges in contemporary education. As you are about to discover, this book is both a powerful inspiration and an invaluable practical resource for making that happen.

Sir Ken Robinson

Transforming school design

Schools, teachers and their pupils will have to adapt as the twenty-first century enters its third decade

Schools and local communities have the responsibility to prepare young people for both a local and a global future. We must, therefore, develop approaches to provide a truly twenty-first-century learning experience. These approaches must shape the design of the spaces and places where learning takes place.

In the introduction to its report 'What Makes a School a Learning Organisation?' the Organisation for Economic Co-operation and Development (OECD) stated: 'Today's schools must equip students with the knowledge and skills they'll need to succeed in an uncertain, constantly changing tomorrow.' And they observed what is universally recognized: '…many schools look the same today as they did a generation ago and they are not developing the pedagogies and practices required to meet the diverse needs of twenty-first century learners.'

The OECD described a learning organization as 'a place where the beliefs, values and norms of employees are brought to bear in support of sustained learning; where a learning atmosphere, learning culture or learning climate is nurtured and where "learning to learn" is essential for everyone.' In describing the development of learning organizations, the OECD has recognized the way in which the organization model has been adopted by many commercial businesses.

The OECD places student learning at the centre of its approach; it believes that schools need to be reconceptualized so that they can embrace innovation and organizational change, improve student outcomes for all students and appropriately prepare the citizens of the future. What is a school if it is not an organization with learning as its core purpose?

There is global acceptance that students now and in the future will need both knowledge and personal/social skills. We have a far greater understanding now of how the brain works and its relationship with the body. The importance of educational technologies to enhance learning, along with developing our understanding and application of artificial intelligence (AI), all have an impact on shaping learning futures.

Many of the contributors to this publication are 'thought leaders' interested in future learning; they share a passion for thinking about how we create and structure learning opportunities to meet the current and future needs of young people.

As Sir Ken Robinson, one of our esteemed contributors, observes, 'The fact is that given the challenges we face, education doesn't need to be reformed – it needs to be transformed. The key to this transformation is not to standardize education, but to personalize it to build achievement on discovering the individual talents of each child, to put students in an environment where they want to learn and where they can naturally discover their true passions.'

Opposite
Responding to a range of learning needs. Freemans Bay, Auckland, NZ

To achieve this, there is a need to move away from the polarized debates of the past that focused on a 'one-size-fits-all' approach to learning and teaching. The future must focus on making learning personal by fully engaging the young person, as an equal, in decisions about their education.

The graphic opposite, *Designing the Pedagogy of Space*, sets out many of the accepted trends that have been identified as influencing and shaping a twenty-first century learning experience. It is not a definitive listing, but it shows the importance of understanding the relationships between pedagogy, the intended curriculum experience, the organization of learning and teaching, and the design of learning spaces.

Personalized learning as a concept has become an established part of educational thinking and development over recent years. Practitioners have recognized the importance of actively designing and planning their teaching around the needs of students. The challenge is that this approach cannot always fully meet the needs of all students. This failing has often resulted in a process of teacher direction with a lack of student engagement in determining need, prior understanding and motivation.

In order to address this issue and engage with and respond to the needs of students, many teachers now work on a more collaborative basis with groups of students. This has created greater flexibility and engagement, opening up new ways of working with students and allowing them to enhance their learning. It also empowers the students to take advantage of a greater choice of where, when and how to learn, thus extending their personal control over the direction and style of their learning.

A curriculum of the past could be said to have been dominated by content coverage, directed by the teacher. The learning experience for the future must move towards a meaningful and creative world for the student, enabled by the teacher. An agenda for learning must motivate and engage, be inclusive and open to collaboration between the school and its community, and be relevant for all learners.

Educators, designers and all others involved in children's future learning must consider these trends when reimagining the design of spaces and places in which students and teachers learn and work.

Designing the pedagogy of space: spaces to encourage creativity and movement

PEDAGOGY CHANGES

Enable learners to see the wider context of their enquiries

CURRICULUM IMPLICATIONS

Learning experiences relevant to real-life/world contexts

IMPLICATIONS FOR DESIGN

Global connectivity; subject adjacencies to improve collaboration; adaptable and reconfigurable space

---

PEDAGOGY CHANGES

Responding to personal learning needs (academic and social)

CURRICULUM IMPLICATIONS

Focus on individuals' skills and competencies to support learning

IMPLICATIONS FOR DESIGN

Spaces for students to work autonomously and receive peer and mentor support

---

PEDAGOGY CHANGES

Modelling learning behaviours

CURRICULUM IMPLICATIONS

Students and teachers share, plan and reflect on learning approaches

IMPLICATIONS FOR DESIGN

Adaptable space for pair and small-group work

PEDAGOGY CHANGES

Collaborative learning

CURRICULUM IMPLICATIONS

Group/team activity in which individual contributions are valued

IMPLICATIONS FOR DESIGN

Variety of spaces to promote team interaction and debate

PEDAGOGY CHANGES

Enquiry-based learning

CURRICULUM IMPLICATIONS

Investigation and exploration, responsive to student learning need

IMPLICATIONS FOR DESIGN

Spaces for researching and testing for individuals and groups

---

PEDAGOGY CHANGES

Thematic and project-based approaches adding depth to learning

CURRICULUM IMPLICATIONS

Interdisciplinary learning, exploring, creating and testing

IMPLICATIONS FOR DESIGN

Studio spaces, shared cross-faculty resource spaces

PEDAGOGY CHANGES

Review, reflection and evidence-based learning

CURRICULUM IMPLICATIONS

Access to, and availability of, data

IMPLICATIONS FOR DESIGN

Quiet, individual and paired spaces, appropriate infrastructure and acoustics

---

PEDAGOGY CHANGES

Practical applications for learning

CURRICULUM IMPLICATIONS

Practical exploration, vocational/industry experience

IMPLICATIONS FOR DESIGN

Appropriate spaces for facilitating work with external partners

Crucial Choices

HOW TO APPROACH SCHOOL DESIGN

Engaging a whole community is the key to developing a school that is fit for the future and reflects new ways of learning

Learning environments are exciting places to design. They are complex public buildings – often the first public buildings that young children will experience. They need to sit centrally and proudly in the community and provide a homely, nurturing space for students. The needs of twenty-first century learning mean that bringing these elements together has become more of a challenge. Architects are designing spaces that do not reflect the learning environment that they personally experienced, and are creating spaces for new activities that are yet to be fully developed or even imagined. New technologies constantly change the requirements of these spaces.

Just as students and teachers need to acquire new skills for the modern world, so too do architects. New ways need to be found to engage the whole school community. Learning environments around the world show that pedagogy, curriculum, society, staffing and politics all influence the design. There is no single template for the design of schools: designs need to respond to each school's unique ethos and context. However, one fundamental design element appears time and again: a rich variety of spaces that gives teachers and students greater choices in how they want to teach and learn. The right configuration of spaces can truly act as a catalyst for change, promoting the benefits of working collaboratively and creatively, letting students take ownership of their environment and helping school communities to deliver the curriculum in new ways.

Observation is a fundamental part of the design process. Designers must look at how spaces and resources are used and how a change of spatial arrangement could improve the learning environment, opening up new and unimagined opportunities.

The school experience is about 'growing human beings'. Schools are not only about learning and teaching but should also provide spaces that encourage young people to become engaged members of a community. The dining spaces must be pleasant and encourage discussion; locker areas should have good levels of passive supervision; and there should be sufficient space both within and outside the school for young people to make choices about how they spend their social time.

Discussing the learning environment will enable and encourage change within the school both for students and teachers. But change doesn't happen immediately, and the environment must not be too challenging for the school community who will need time to absorb and adapt to change. Transformation is therefore often effected by small steps.

Architects are partners in the creation of the new space and should challenge and stimulate dialogue around it. They should open the school community's eyes to the art of the possible; they are not there to write the education brief, but to respond to the school's requirements. Architects should take their time getting to know the schools they work with – not only the physical constraints, but also the culture and vision for the future. The people involved in the project may have

Opposite
The journey through school design. Bedales School Orchard Development, Hampshire, UK

HOW TO APPROACH SCHOOL DESIGN

little experience of working with architects, so it is useful to develop a common language from the start – through conversation, visits to relevant buildings, and workshops.

It is important to consider, for example: What does innovation look like for this school? Do we all understand the meaning of hubs, pods and breakout spaces? Would it be useful to mock up a space to understand its size and how it may work? Is the school using the building project as a catalyst for change? Architects have found that in-depth focus meetings are a good way to engage a large number of people at once, for briefing and sharing initial ideas.

It is the architect's role to fully analyse the site and buildings, then respond to constraints and turn them into opportunities. Typical constraints that architects face may include the following:

- Budgetary: repurposing existing buildings often results in interesting learning environments and will create less disruption during construction.

- Topography: a sloping/stepped site can be used to create multiple levels, amphitheatre stairs and other outdoor learning spaces.

- Making the most of outdoor spaces: even in cooler climates, outdoor space should be an extension of the learning environment, as defined and varied as indoor spaces.

- Safety of pupils when working on occupied school sites: provided the safety of the school community is the top priority, a building programme can be a wonderful learning tool for the students and stakeholders.

- Poorly defined brief: while some schools believe they should arrive with a full brief, architects can get a deeper understanding of a school's requirements when they are part of the team defining the brief.

Below
Extending inside/outside learning. Royal Botanic Gardens, London, UK

HOW TO APPROACH SCHOOL DESIGN

Right
Scale models can improve understanding of the space being designed

Key considerations for the best learning environment

- Ensure 'buy-in' from all staff; without this the design will fail.

- Create a comfortable environment – get the basics right.

- Enable smooth, easy flow between spaces.

- Develop a common language between designers and staff; discuss what works and what doesn't. Agree on what changes need to be made to enhance a new way of learning, and the considerations of the individual school.

- Recognize the importance of undefined space (that is, not the classrooms, offices and so on) – the 'glue' where learning and socializing interact.

- Create mock-ups to test ideas before building them.

- Use all available tools to explain ideas clearly to the many people involved in the project, the majority of whom might not understand how to 'read' drawings, proportion or space.

- Visualize a day in the life of a student, teacher, parent and the leadership and support teams.

- Remember that the outdoors is as important as the indoors.

Advice to designers

- Take time to research best practice from around the world and the opportunities provided by changing technologies.

- Spend time in schools observing the link between pedagogy and space.

- Develop your communication skills.

- Design environments that can be used in ways that were never imagined.

HOW TO APPROACH SCHOOL DESIGN

What characterizes the learning culture you are aiming for?

CONSCIOUS

Artefacts
Observable objects and behaviours

A typical example rooted in a 20th-century learning model	Learning at Høsterkøb School, Denmark

Sit down. Be quiet. Listen, and speak only when asked. Don't move around. Do what everybody else is doing.	Focus on the personalized task at hand. Find a place that works well for you. You can move around, work with peers and change your learning strategy if needed.

SUBCONSCIOUS

Values and beliefs
Not directly observable, but is experienced and understood from how people explain and justify what they do

We all learn in the same way and should learn the same things at the same time. The teacher is the main source of knowledge.	We have different needs and preferences that help us learn well. We learn at our own pace and can help each other learn.

Based on Edgar Schein, Organizational Culture

HOW TO BEGIN

Before you begin, understand that learning spaces are an expression of a learning culture and design them to strengthen that culture

Open a classroom door, and you will often find around 25 identical desks. That's 25 identical work stations for 25 different students, all of whom have different needs and preferences. They will all be at different stages in their learning, and with different life paths ahead of them. The learning culture expressed through this layout and choice of furniture doesn't meet the needs of twenty-first century learning. Yet, this teacher-centred model of instruction has become the predominant one driving school design.

Research clearly shows that lecture-style teaching is one of the least effective ways for students to learn. As a general rule, a student is able to pay attention to and recall what is being said for the same number of minutes as his or her age. This means that the amount of time that a student in a class will benefit from this style of teaching will be between 5 and 15 minutes at the most. And yet, currently, most classrooms are designed for this type of instruction. Instead, classrooms should be designed for the way we know learning works, and for nurturing those skills and competences that are needed today.

Be conscious of the power of spaces in shaping actions and behaviour. Spaces affect the way we think, feel and act – and this obviously applies to students and teachers. A classroom laid out in rows sets the scene for a traditional teacher-centred instruction. To prepare young people for the future will require new approaches to learning and teaching. To meet young people's individual needs, learning must be more engaging, relevant and personal. Do our spaces communicate and encourage what we wish to see in our schools?

A helpful model to analyse and reflect on spaces in schools is based on Edgar Schein's model of organizational culture (opposite). Consider the characteristics of the learning culture that are implicit in the design and organization of space.

What do teachers want when it comes to school and learning space design? They first and foremost want their ideas and thoughts to be heard. And when the spaces are conceived collaboratively, learning spaces can become inclusive, welcoming environments that support learning and well-being for all children.

The fundamental conditions of the space

The fundamental conditions of the space – good acoustics, a positive atmosphere, natural light and a choice of materials and colours that help to communicate the values of the school – are of huge importance. To create a welcoming place you must consider the layout, the range and the style of furniture that is provided for students. For example, focused light in a larger space creates the illusion of separate smaller spaces, which in turn helps to increase concentration and lower noise levels.

HOW TO BEGIN

Designing for learning – creating functions and zones

Learning spaces should reflect the learning activities as well as offer a choice to students. Zones should be designed for different functions:

- Instruction and presentation.

- Collaboration.

- Quiet study.

- Creative production.

- Social interaction.

- Access to the external environment.

Different age groups, different cultures and different countries may require additional zones. For example, in Denmark physical movement is an integral part of learning so zones for movement and play would be integral to the design.

CONSIDERATIONS

- Teaching staff should be included in key discussions.

- There should be a focus on the shared vision, values and learning philosophy.

- What are the long-term goals?

- Engage with the students. What works for them? What different needs do they have?

- Consider and respond to individual learning needs (academic and social) in the planning.

- Be clear about the why, the how and the what of the learning space design.

- Review appropriate research.

- Ensure stakeholders are engaged and invested.

- Use inspiring examples to develop collective thinking.

HOW TO BEGIN

Crucial choices – what should be the initial focus?

A great learning environment is the physical representation of a well-functioning learning culture – the values, beliefs and pedagogical practices shared by teachers and students. When spaces and culture are in harmony, the spaces actively support learning and thus support the goals of the school.

The design should be driven by the learning philosophy, and the initial areas for questions the architect should ask are as follows:

1. Vision and values

Understand the school's values, beliefs and desired future pedagogical practices. This is the basis of the vision for the future. This is a collaborative process, so involve as many teachers as possible.

- Where does the school want to be in 5, 10, 15 years' time?

- What legacy does the school want to leave?

- What does learning ideally look like, and how are the roles of both students and teachers changing?

- How best can the students be supported?

Use inspirational examples – from the field of education or otherwise. Be aware of neurology and learning research.

2. Pedagogy and activities

The next step is to establish how learning should ideally take place.

- What activities should be happening?

- What functions are needed by teachers and by students?

- How are learners' needs being met?

- What choices are being provided for the students?

- How should the students feel and how should they be encouraged to act?

These questions help to focus the conversation around pedagogical practice that can later be interpreted into physical forms.

It is beneficial at this point to engage with the students and ask:

- Where and how do they feel they work most effectively, both at school and at home? And why?

- What do they prefer to do during breaks?

- In what type of environment are they most comfortable?

3. Organizing learning

Next clarify who needs to work with whom and when, in order to establish the general layout of the learning environment.

- How will group sizes vary throughout the day?

- How should the different functions and groups be organized?

- Will students be organized by class, year group or otherwise?

- How should areas be integrated with each other?

- Will there be classrooms, or a more flexible open or semi-open learning hub?

HOW TO BEGIN

Making sense – why and how to co-create

Great learning environments enhance both learning and teaching. The short-cut to creating one is to co-create with the teachers, in collaborative, hands-on ways that help to build a collective understanding of future pedagogical practices.

Great projects, great 'buy-in'?

Some new school projects with exciting new designs somehow do not fulfil their promise. How is it that some schools that have been designed with brilliant ideas, the latest practice and even research and evidence still turn out to be a challenge? This is a problem so common that it is addressed regularly at international conferences on school design. The building is not being used as envisaged by the architects and designers. The teachers struggle to make the spaces work for them and the architects complain about the teachers' lack of vision and willingness to adapt. Thus, teachers put storage furniture in front of retractable walls and large posters cover transparent surfaces in an attempt to recreate a familiar space.

There is a gap to be bridged between those who design the spaces and those who use the spaces, so that ultimately the learning environment makes sense for those who use it.

Making sense is simply about finding the right solution. It is a process. The brain relies on pattern recognition. Once something is out of key with our known patterns, there is a natural resistance until a new understanding or pattern has manifested itself in a meaningful way. Try crossing your arms, and then cross them the opposite way. It doesn't feel natural or comfortable. Teachers need to be involved in the process of reshaping their mental patterns and developing their understanding of what future learning practices could look like.

Building a school or (re)designing learning spaces is therefore a process of both developing physical solutions and pedagogical practice, while engaging with the teachers.

Experience shows that it is simply not enough to communicate frequently and ensure that everybody has heard or read about the ideas behind new school design. People have to be engaged. As with learning, it has to be an active process in order for new patterns and understandings to become established. There is a far higher chance of success if teachers are actively involved in the key design stages of this journey.

Less talk, more action

Opposite
A scale model brings
real engagement

The way in which the design solution is developed and defined is crucial. Working hands-on – creating simple prototypes and developing shared ideas and an understanding of how future learning spaces could look and function – is the most effective way for architects and educators or teachers to act together.

HOW SPACE CAN PROVOKE LEARNING

When planning learning spaces in schools, explore the wonderful opportunities that creating a new space can bring in terms of learning, community and culture

A space with its inhabitants forms a dynamic ecology. It is not always clear how much a space influences behaviour, but imagine playing rugby in a church and it is clear that the space might be more significant than is perhaps recognized.

When designing a new learning space there is a tendency to focus on fixing existing problems rather than creating a space that most purposefully supports a new vision. Habitually, teachers will set up their rooms in a certain manner and they often remain that way, rather than adapt to accommodate the changing needs of learners day to day. Teachers often unconsciously teach with an imaginary version of themselves in mind. It makes intuitive sense that this is the right way to do something because it evolves from how the teacher thinks.

Thus, teaching and engaging with students who present a challenge can be where the greatest potential for learning occurs for the teacher. The same self-referencing process might be said to apply when designing learning spaces – the space that is created suits the individual who created it, but potentially stifles the learning of others.

The Plymouth School of Creative Arts in the UK was designed as a school with 'making' in mind. The vision for the school was one where creative arts could be practised anywhere. This resulted in the adoption of concrete floors for practical reasons, where creative and applied learning could easily take place within all learning and teaching environments. This changed the way the school decided to describe its learning spaces, with a conscious choice of the word 'studios' rather than 'classrooms'. A teacher entering a studio rather than a classroom would have different expectations for teaching maths, geography and other subjects to pupils ranging from nursery age through to 16-year-old students.

New expectations created new possibilities. Just as the artist structures their studio to create work, so the teachers tailored their studios to ensure learning happened. This inspired a completely different perspective. From the initial design intentions to how the school ultimately lives and works in the space, new possibilities emerged.

Opposite
Space for movement and
creativity. Plymouth School
of Creative Arts, Plymouth, UK

HOW SPACE CAN PROVOKE LEARNING

In the open-plan studios of the Plymouth School of Creative Arts, important professional development is happening each day within the learning teams that have been established. The collaborative nature of the space has creatively provoked learning. This is not always comfortable for teachers at first; teachers feel that they should be in control, even though it is clear that you cannot control learning. But stepping beyond those fears – those boundaries that can limit potential – allows the learning to be enhanced in new ways.

By recognizing that learning needs to shift gear and prepare students for a rapidly changing world, and not just an exam, there is a need to move past old educational practices and to innovate. A project- and enquiry-based approach requires a different pedagogy where students can immerse themselves, research, experiment, make and present. It is imperative to see that space, inhabitants and pedagogy are all interdependent and complementary.

It is essential to ensure that students and staff learn in inspiring spaces with a rich pedagogy and curriculum. For an educational designer uncertainty can be both unnerving and exciting, but it must be embraced. One way of embracing this challenge is to consider the question: 'What can this space provoke in our learning?'

Opposite
BYOP – Bring Your Own Plant to school. St Francis Xavier College, Officer, Melbourne, Australia

---

CONSIDERATIONS

- What is the purpose of the current layout of your learning space?

- Whose needs does the learning space serve?

- What do you want the space to enable?

- How should the space reflect the culture and ethos of the school?

- How dynamic and adaptable is your current learning space?

- What are your sources of inspiration?

- How can you make your learning space more dynamic and adaptable for future learning?

- Open and collaborative spaces need clarity of roles and leadership for all staff and students.

HOW TO ENGAGE LEARNERS

Adaptable and dynamic learning zones can engage learners in so many different ways

Externally, West Thornton Primary Academy, in London, UK, looks like a traditional Victorian building typical of so many schools in England. However, the inside is anything but traditional. Over a five-year period the school went on a transformative journey from box classrooms to modern, open-plan, flexible learning zones. In these spaces, up to 90 children learn together all day with a team of staff, either in small focus groups, collaboratively with friends or by themselves.

Why change?

The staff were driven by a concern that the children's education was not preparing them for life in the twenty-first century and that they had needs other than just reaching an expected level in standardized tests. As a large and diverse primary school – its 850 pupils were drawn from homes where 39 different languages are spoken – in a deprived part of London, the staff felt there needed to be a more meaningful and engaging curriculum experience for their pupils.

There was a recognition that the teachers were exhausting themselves trying to help the pupils to reach the necessary standards; conversely, it seemed that the greater the teachers' efforts to support the pupils, the less the pupils did for themselves. The teachers were the hardest-working people in the room and it had become clear that change was needed.

Pedagogy and space

The school began a large-scale curriculum review – aiming for creativity and relevance – in the hope it would lead to children having greater engagement in, and ownership of, learning. An ethos of 'challenge' was developed in the school, making sure all children understood that there was no learning without struggle, and that learning success should be celebrated.

Opportunities were introduced for children to make choices in their work and more group activities were planned. These approaches – offering learners more control – began to have a visible impact on their progress.

Staff began to address critical questions concerning the way current and future learning should be developed. They wanted the children to be resilient, independent and collaborative learners, and to be aspirational and confident about their own futures. Staff recognized the importance of the relationship between pedagogy and space in developing this approach. Through intensive observation and data collection it was evident that the separate, traditional, closed design of groups of classroom spaces was constraining a range of learning activities and experiences.

Opposite above
How are you going to bring the outside in?

Opposite below
Go to the pit to solve the problem.

Both pictures: West Thornton Primary Academy, London, UK

HOW TO ENGAGE LEARNERS

Design for purpose

In the new spaces that were developed, pupils were offered choice: choice over where to sit, who to work with, in what order to do their work, what level of challenge they were ready for and how they wanted to demonstrate their learning. Only hard work, deadlines and high standards were not a choice.

Furniture in the spaces was largely flexible and could be moved by the children to suit their purposes; there were no fixed areas for different subjects. The spaces were designed to allow the sharing of ideas, to encourage talk and to aid collaboration. Writeable surfaces (such as tables, walls and windows) abounded, encouraging children to share their ideas and take learning risks in public. Tiered seating provided opportunities for different-sized groups to listen, receive instruction or demonstrate to each other. Different seating choices in the zones ranged from tables and chairs of differing heights to cushions and sofas, creating a sense of homeliness and comfort. Learners were encouraged to choose the most appropriate seating and space for the task in hand. At the same time, each zone was designed to offer some private, quieter spaces suitable for focus work, independent work or filming and recording. Integrated ICT (information and communications technology) played a large role in these spaces, with options for learners to switch freely between mobile devices such as laptops or iPads. The use of apps and learning platforms blurred the line between learning at home and at school.

The design of the zones had just as powerful an effect on the teachers, forcing them to behave differently too. The spaces were more suited to small-group teaching because there was no front of the room that a teacher could dominate. The flexible and open nature of the space meant that collaboration with colleagues was both necessary and easy to achieve. Not every teacher could immediately adapt to working in this way. However, no teacher who has worked in the zones wishes to go back in a box. They have found it supportive to work alongside other teachers and have been inspired by the way the children responded to taking control.

Below
West Thornton Primary
Academy, London, UK

Right
West Thornton Primary
Academy, London, UK

Overleaf
Discovery Elementary School,
Arlington, VA, USA

Learning and teaching gains

The design and operation of the learning zones has had a direct and powerful impact on improving learning outcomes. There have also been other unexpected benefits to working in this way:

- Attendance rose above the national average for the first time.

- Behaviour improved, with low-level disruption in the classroom effectively disappearing. It also improved in the playground because there was no longer an explosion of pent-up energy from children who had been forced to restrict their movements in the classroom.

- Use of technology as well as increased motivation has led to greater participation in home learning tasks.

- The teachers from the high schools that the pupils have moved on to always comment on the positive learning behaviours of the West Thornton children.

To date, the school has found that their children are ready to take on, enjoy and succeed in whatever challenge they are offered. They have encapsulated their experiences in the newly adopted West Thornton Primary Academy mantra: 'Children will constantly surprise you… but only if you let them.'

CONSIDERATIONS

- How are you preparing your primary learners for more meaningful and engaging twenty-first century learning?

- What value do you place on younger learners taking responsibility for their learning and being active participants in the process?

- Is the vision and ethos of the school reflected in the day-to-day learning experience?

- How should a learning space look in order to encourage collaboration, independence, enquiry, creativity and responsibility?

- What can you draw from current research into learning and teaching to enhance the design of new environments for learning?

- In what ways are other countries designing new learning spaces to meet new needs?

- Why are forward-thinking international organizations providing spaces that give their people voice and choice in their day-to-day working environment?

The Learning Journey

DESIGNING FOR PRE-SCHOOL AND EARLY YEARS

Play is a crucial motivation when children first start school, and a creative and imaginative physical space will motivate younger learners and enable new kinds of interactions

The Rosan Bosch Studio in Copenhagen has led the way in the design of physical spaces in early and primary years education. Working as a team of artists, architects, designers and academics, its goal is to create designs that change behaviour in these pre-school and early years phases.

Design can be used as a strategic tool to encourage people to act differently – to change their behaviour, to prompt them to communicate in new ways or to engage in creative activities or play. In this way, design can help new and more efficient learning scenarios to develop.

Imagine the school as being made up of three connected components: the organization, the pedagogy and the design of the physical environment. Together, the three components form what the students experience as the culture of their school – how they are taught, who conducts the class and where it all happens. This approach is applied in many countries throughout the world and is central to the design thinking that underlies the planning of learning spaces as set out in this book.

All three components have to be involved when creating progressive learning spaces. If one component is neglected, a change of culture is not really embedded. The teachers must feel enthusiastic about using the space and its facilities as educational tools, while the organization should adapt its planning, schedules, student arrangements and general working conditions for teachers, making it easy to conduct classes on a day-to-day basis.

Unfortunately, school building projects seldom begin with the need to shape the school's culture or aid its pedagogy. Instead, new schools are often built according to a list of necessities based primarily on the organization's need. For example, if a school must accommodate 200 children, the architects would begin by deciding the required number of classrooms, corridors, toilets and seating places. The design would develop to match these objectives – resulting inevitably in a school that replicates those built many times before; that is, one where the interior does not support engaging ways of learning.

The design process must work from the inside out, and evolve by looking at what motivates and empowers learners and teachers. Although there are many constantly evolving learning methods, no one learns well by being continuously in the same mode – for example, sitting at a desk receiving one-way information.

Opposite
A learning landscape. Liceo Europa, Zaragoza, Spain

DESIGNING FOR PRE-SCHOOL AND EARLY YEARS

Instead, each learner needs to access a variety of learning environments and situations which engage both the mind and the body. Students' learning needs differ according to the tasks in question, the time of day and whether it is an individual assignment, group project or a more practical learning activity.

Translating needs into design principles

In the book *Campfires in Cyberspace: Primordial Metaphors for Learning in the 21st Century*, author and futurist David Thornburg describes digital learning in terms of the features of a prehistoric landscape, such as watering holes and places for campfires. These features work as an inspiration for many architects and have been further developed into learning-based design practices – for example, the six design principles for learning situations by Rosan Bosch Studio:

- Mountaintop – for practising presentation skills.

- Cave – a sheltered space for concentrating.

- Campfire – for smaller teams to focus on discussion, storytelling and debate.

- Watering hole – a place for informal learning with peer-engagement.

- Hands-on – a design principle that recognizes the value of sensory learning experiences through exploring or practical prototyping.

- Movement – physical activities that enhance cognitive skills.

Each principle enables and supports a learning scenario shaped by the degree of contact with other learners. Some spatial concepts direct and concentrate attention, while others harness the energy of the children.

Opposite above
Gathering below the mountain top. Liceo Europa, Zaragoza, Spain

Categorizing learning spaces

Identifying the diversity of learning needs and scenarios enables us to better plan learning spaces. The larger spatial categories within the school will need to support several of the design principles to offer flexible and differentiated learning spaces. For example, an open space with a 'mountaintop' design for instructing a group of students that also allows it to be used at other times for 'watering hole' and 'movement' activities.

To start planning these spatial categories and destinations within the school, it can work well to consider a mixed degree of openness to the surroundings – from private and semi-private to entirely open spaces. This creates new spatial dynamics and takes advantage of unused space for corridors and transit areas.

All schools will require their unique categories to be tailored to the specific needs of their learners' age and needs, pedagogy and resources, while also recognizing their local surroundings and practices.

Allowing the spatial categories to evolve from the design principles avoids reproducing traditional classrooms. Instead, the design is created from the inside out, based on the learners' needs.

Opposite below
Caves come in all shapes and sizes. The Sheikh Zayed Private Academy, Abu Dhabi, UAE

DESIGNING FOR PRE-SCHOOL AND EARLY YEARS

Pre-school: belonging to a neighbourhood

For younger children there are specific considerations to acknowledge – the sense of 'where do I belong?' This is particularly important when working with pre-schoolers because they need a sense of their own space, a place where they feel safe and at home.

Traditionally, children's need to belong has been fulfilled by the walls of the classroom, so generally schools have classrooms and few common areas. But the classroom and the place where the child feels at home do not have to be the same thing. Instead, it is possible to create 'neighbourhoods' to which the child belongs. Everyone is welcome in a neighbourhood – other children can come to work, play or socialize.

The older the children get, the more adventurous they become, and the structure opens up. Growing up is about exploring, but children grow up at different paces and the desire to explore is not the same for all, so a neighbourhood must support the needs of all the children.

Learning outside in pre-school

Outdoor learning opens up a new realm of possibilities, so it is important to break down the boundaries between interior and exterior environments.

The design principle of 'movement' is an obvious part of outdoor learning for pre-school students. Wide open spaces are great for running, jumping and skipping, but being outside is also beneficial for other learning scenarios, so give more room for hiding, for searching and exploring. The design principle of 'hands-on' is given a whole new lease of life when set within the diversity of nature.

The outdoors is an accessible and inexpensive way to make more space available. If the learning environment incorporates the outside space, it allows the students the opportunity to be more creative. They get the freedom to construct, build and adapt their learning space – either in reality or using their imagination.

The interior learning space must be connected to the outdoor areas, so the choice to go outside is always available. The variety of environments will motivate and inspire pre-school students to think differently about maths or learning languages. The outside space requires little work – all that is needed is shade for schools in sunny climates and shelter for schools in colder ones.

Opposite
A real campfire. Høsterkøb
School, Høsterkøb, Denmark

DESIGNING FOR PRE-SCHOOL AND EARLY YEARS

Primary school – learning is a social process

Human beings are social, which means that a lot of skills develop through the interaction with others. When 50 primary students get together, they will learn most effectively with or from their peers. Learning is a social process that enables them to share, discuss, observe and copy methods to try on their own. The physical design of the educational space is about enabling them to get together, so they can communicate, engage and learn with and from each other.

Skills for the twenty-first century involve social abilities – knowing how to deal with other people. How do I contribute to get my group to do better? Not just me, but also the others in the group? This means that the school day should not be structured around the teacher-to-student distribution of information. Instead, educators take on the role of guide in the learning community, so that student-to-student interaction plays a more significant part of the learning process.

It is vital to create learning spaces where the environment encourages different behaviour patterns from everyone – both students and teachers.

Learning outside in primary

Today's students need to be outdoors more than ever. The outside environment supports children's health and development in every major way – academically, emotionally, socially and physically.

Often playgrounds are paved over with asphalt and tend to focus on organized play and sports. The outdoor environment is seldom used as one of the school's main learning spaces. But for primary students, nature can be the source of countless learning opportunities. Children become absorbed planting seeds, seeing flowers grow, producing vegetables, pulling worms from the earth, watching butterflies swarm around flowers and measuring water from rain barrels. They are applying the skills developed in maths, science and a range of subjects while simultaneously becoming familiar with ecosystems, pollination and weather cycles.

Students enjoy learning in outdoor learning environments – and teachers will too. But for school organizations, taking teaching outside is a significant challenge. It requires great courage and ambition to change learning from something that takes place in a classroom to an activity that can unfold anywhere.

In designing primary schools, the importance of ease of access to the external learning environment has been a central consideration. In many primary schools that are more than single storey, outside terraces – learning platforms – have been added to each floor to enable the learning environment at each floor level to achieve this access.

Opposite
Learning deep, mountain high. The Vittra Telefonplan School, Stockholm, Sweden

Below
The Vittra Telefonplan School creates a flexible and dynamic learning landscape, where both fixed and moveable workshop destinations make the school adaptable to individual learning needs

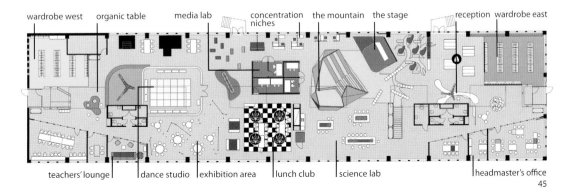

wardrobe west   organic table   media lab   concentration niches   the mountain   the stage   reception   wardrobe east

teachers' lounge   dance studio   exhibition area   lunch club   science lab   headmaster's office

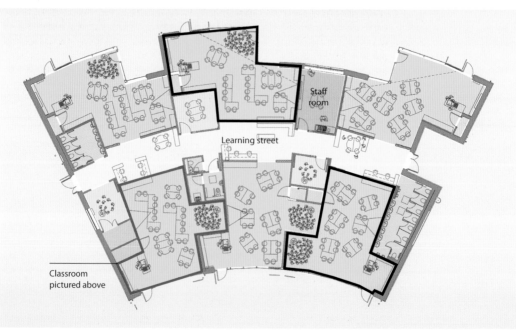

Staff room

Learning street

Classroom
pictured above

DESIGNING THE PRIMARY LANDSCAPE

There is more to a classroom than a square box

All teachers are aware of the potential in all children and the importance of creating a structured approach that acknowledges the different levels of understanding in each child. At the same time, teachers recognize that creativity, enquiry and personal choice – based on when, where and how to learn – are paramount.

The space within schools is often described as the 'third teacher', an expression first used after the Second World War by Loris Malaguzzi, the founder and director of the renowned municipal pre-schools of Reggio Emilia, Italy. Malaguzzi's 'third teacher' is a flexible environment, responsive to the need for teachers and children to create learning together. Value is placed on developing a learning environment that is both teacher-enabled and learner-directed.

These approaches are causing primary schools to rethink the pattern and design of learning spaces. There is greater recognition of new learning needs and a move away from the standardized approach with the rethinking of the 'classroom' as a semi-open rather than a closed space.

The reshaping of the traditional classroom space to accommodate a wider range of learning scenarios is being established throughout the world. This has led to the implementation of larger and more connected spaces – as illustrated earlier – where teams of teachers work in collaboration with larger groups of learners.

Architect Herman Hertzberger, a contributor to this book, identified two different types of classroom that enable very different styles of teaching.

The first is a basic rectangular classroom, which Hertzberger described as unarticulated. The shape promotes instruction from a teacher directly to pupils who will all be within their view. This is a very traditional model and will be familiar to most. Changing the shape of the classroom to a more irregular space creates different spaces for learning within the overall classroom design (see below), allowing for a wider range of learning activities. Hertzberger described this as an articulated space, which provides more opportunity for children to work independently in nooks and corners, or in a range of adaptable groups and settings organized by the teacher. Here, the number of learning and teaching options is greater, allowing the teacher to operate from many locations within the space.

Opposite above and below
The articulated classroom from concept to reality. University of Cambridge Primary School, Cambridge, UK

Unarticulated classroom

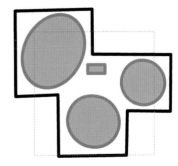

Articulated classroom

DESIGNING THE PRIMARY LANDSCAPE

This effect was particularly noted in primary schools, where pupils spend longer periods of time within their 'home', or class, teaching base. Bringing together articulated classroom spaces can easily enable new learning connections in new learning landscapes.

Articulated classrooms are particularly noticeable in the University of Cambridge Primary School (UCPS) designed by Julia Barfield of Marks Barfield Architects (pictured on page 46).

The development of more open and connected spaces not only provides a greater range of learning opportunities (see opposite), but also allows much easier planning and design of the connections between inside and outside learning environments. This allows for a more diverse learning experience and also offers new and motivational opportunities outside, thereby providing not only practical experience but also enabling the learner to understand and relate to the local community.

A good example of this approach is the development, in many countries, of Forest Schools, where a woodland environment means the learning experience is enhanced by simultaneously fostering scientific enquiry and research into local and natural habitats, and engaging with the outside world.

CONSIDERATIONS

• Are you developing your learning spaces to promote creativity, enquiry and exploration?

• Are you ensuring that your learning spaces are designed to support physical activity and movement throughout the school day?

• Are you creating a learning environment that acknowledges collaborative learning?

• Are you designing a complementary range of spaces to ensure you encourage a wider and more diverse range of personal learning activities for your children?

• Are you providing adaptable and reconfigurable spaces that can respond to the changing needs of students?

• Are you establishing visual transparency between connected learning spaces?

• Are you making good connections to outdoor play and learning areas?

Opposite
The full landscape – inside/outside learning with strong internal connections. Lairdsland Primary School, Kirkintilloch, Scotland, UK

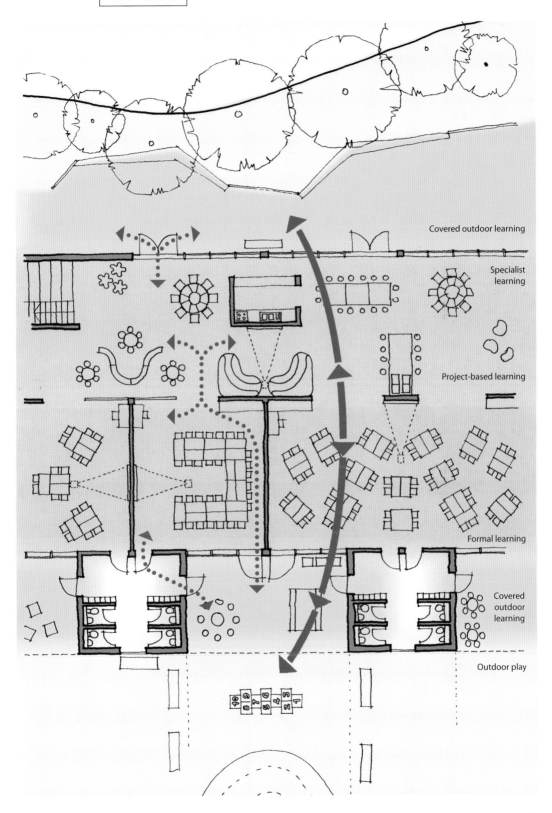

Covered outdoor learning

Specialist learning

Project-based learning

Formal learning

Covered outdoor learning

Outdoor play

DESIGNING FOR THE TRANSITION TO SECONDARY AND BEYOND

Flexibility is a buzzword in modern education and learning spaces can benefit from it. But to rely on it as the 'be all and end all' is not the answer

Architects who have been involved for many years in the design of education spaces regularly hear the request for flexible teaching spaces, usually from teachers trying to define the spaces that will enable them to deliver the 'teaching'. It is the default mindset for how to improve upon the traditional classroom. We all know we need to move on from the traditional classroom model, and invoking the F-word – flexibility – is assumed to be the key to this.

For over a century the needs of the industrial model of education have been fulfilled by the traditional classroom, which can work perfectly for didactic teaching. From one perspective, its efficiency is unmatched: a basic classroom typically requires only 2 square metres (21.5 square feet) of space per student, while contemporary learning environments will typically require around double that area.

For some learning and teaching activities, the classroom can be an effective delivery vehicle. The classroom will always be part of our learning landscape and the teacher-led mode of instruction still has a role to play. However, the classroom unit in its current form cannot remain the only medium within the new landscapes for twenty-first century learning.

In contemporary learning environments, there should be so much more variety and opportunity to support emerging educational practices and activities. To create these purposeful spaces, we have to first consider how we think about space itself. As the environmental psychologist Robert Bechtel said: 'Behaviour, not space, is enclosed by architecture…' Space has an impact on us and affects our behaviour. Think about how you feel walking into a medieval cathedral – you may be inspired, fall silent or be hushed, be overwhelmed or grow contemplative. Now consider the desired effects that school spaces should have.

Designers, teachers, students, administrators and facility managers all tend to think about space very differently. To the designer, the space is paramount – it must support all the functions briefed or implied, encapsulate the philosophy of the school and inspire its inhabitants. To the teachers, it is the workplace and one that either supports or constrains the delivery of their professional aspirations. To the students, it might be the symbol of the education system, loved or loathed, or it may be the place of friendships and fun. To the administrators, it may simply be the living evocation of the timetable – have I got enough classrooms for this year's curriculum? Facility and business managers will view the space in terms of capital and recurrent costs. These differing perspectives provide a dilemma for designers developing briefs for school spaces.

Opposite
Varied learning spaces.
South Melbourne Primary
School, Australia

DESIGNING FOR THE TRANSITION TO SECONDARY AND BEYOND

How to define contemporary learning space

The design of contemporary learning spaces is inspired by pedagogy. You can't successfully design education spaces unless you fully understand the learning and teaching practices they need to support. It really is that simple.

It is critical for the designer to understand the learning and teaching model that the particular school wants to follow, and then to interpret that into an integrated combination of purposeful settings that enhance and support the model. This requires a clear articulation of the client's education vision, values and teaching practices.

Designers need to start with 'inside-out' design. Establish a clear understanding of the 'why' and the 'how' from the very start, before engaging with the design process. Next, the 'what' – the design responses and the elements required in the form of a functional brief – will define the education 'experience' that is being sought.

Rather than considering the specification of the spaces required, the overall educational 'experience' needs to be defined and clarified with the educators first. Educators may find it difficult to define the learning space they want – it is hard to imagine new models when innovative examples are so few or are unknown.

The 'experience' is informed by four factors: the activities that are expected to take place; what kinds of relationships will be encouraged; how much time will be given over to different activities; and defining the environment that will support the overall experience.

Learning landscapes

Given the complexities of defining the space, an easier way is to imagine a larger landscape that supports multiple opportunities and activities.

A key driver in developing purposeful spaces is to support the flow of learning. Providing varied opportunities for teachers and students allows activities to be connected, active, personal and – most importantly – to be responsive to the needs of the students or staff. However, 'flexible' spaces can lose the immediacy of the moment and the single-focus purpose. Because flexible spaces need to be configured for the specific activity and then deconstructed for the next, there is the risk that the loss of critical time and absence of a single purpose means that such spaces can undermine the flow of learning.

There needs to be a balance between the structured and semi-structured spaces (the purposeful spaces) with other spaces that can be easily manipulated and reconfigured (the agile spaces). These need to be arranged logically to support the flow of learning.

Developing communities of learners and learning communities

Increasingly, our design of learning landscapes focuses on the learning and teaching within 'learning communities', rather than on individual classrooms. Learning communities provide ways of organizing subjects, grouping students and enabling learning activities, while supporting social and academic engagement. Importantly, they can also provide a home base where the students are better known and supported in all aspects of their life and work within the school. Many schools have developed curriculum approaches where teams of staff work for longer periods of time across integrated themes or project-based approaches to develop deeper relationships with groups of learners.

Opposite above
Visual connection between studio and breakout space. Trumpington Community College, Cambridge, UK

Opposite below
Defined spaces for groups to gather. St Francis Xavier College, Officer, Melbourne, Australia

DESIGNING FOR THE TRANSITION TO SECONDARY AND BEYOND

The ideal learning community size can be up to 100 or even 150 students, according to research by the evolutionary psychologist Robin Dunbar. The learning communities themselves can be sub-divided into smaller student groups or 'learning neighbourhoods'. These could equate to traditional class sizes and allow teachers to work in both classroom groups and within larger learning community settings. Importantly, this configuration also speaks to the ideal size of an interdisciplinary, collaborative teacher team of four to six core teachers.

Social scientists have long studied the importance of community. Étienne Wenger's seminal book *Communities of Practice: Learning, Meaning, and Identity* extended the social theory of learning by providing a specific framework for educational design. Importantly for the consideration of designing learning communities, Wenger identified four premises:

- Being social is central to the human experience and therefore vital to learning.

- Knowledge is contextual.

- Knowledge is active.

- Learning must be meaningful.

Opposite
Collaborative learning
in connected spaces.
Brighton Secondary College,
Victoria, Australia

The South Melbourne Primary School in Australia has 525 students. The seven year groups are arranged in learning neighbourhoods of 75 students and three teachers, with two learning neighbourhoods per floor level making up a community of 150 students. This allows the learning community to operate as a year group (age-based) or to operate on a more stage-based or 'vertical' organizational model.

Of course, in the enquiry-based learning model of contemporary education, learning communities should feature:

- Student agency – allowing students to explore their own learning paths.

- Connected learning and teaching opportunities and choices.

- Cross-curricular working.

- 'Home', 'place', security and safety implied as four separate concepts.

- Collaboration with both students and teachers.

- Personalization.

An example of Dunbar's learning neighbourhoods

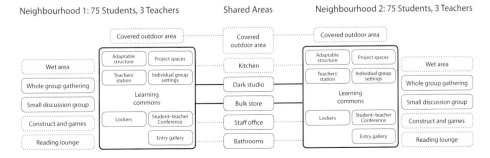

Neighbourhood 1: 75 Students, 3 Teachers   Shared Areas   Neighbourhood 2: 75 Students, 3 Teachers

DESIGNING FOR THE TRANSITION TO SECONDARY AND BEYOND

The learning hub: a secondary experience

Increasingly, the contemporary learning landscape is being applied not only to the primary school (where it is easier to enact) but also to the secondary school (where it is often challenged by the dictates of curriculum-delivery and compliance issues). Tertiary institutions are also increasingly adopting the active, cross-disciplinary model in the form of humanities spaces fused with technology spaces and the emergence of 'maker spaces'. Fundamentally, the philosophies and the principles remain constant across the sectors, although each is responding to slightly different external pressures and, obviously, refining their responses to suit the age requirements of their students.

The work of Caulfield Grammar School in Australia on their Learning Project shows what can be achieved in the secondary school environment. It was developed as a model for a school with traditional facilities but transitioning to more contemporary practices. The Learning Project provided a stand-alone prototype facility to test a wide variety of spatial arrangements designed to provoke innovation in learning and teaching practice.

The Learning Project exhibits a series of purposeful and connected learning settings, each designed to support a particular learning activity. The positioning, size and connectedness of these settings was explored throughout the design process with the school, ensuring the project maximized opportunities for a multi-modal, learner-centred pedagogy. The Caulfield project explores purposeful spaces over flexible ones, where users of the space will intuitively understand the activities the settings are designed to support. By limiting the flexibility of some spaces, the quality of the experience for the user is increased because the lighting, acoustics, furniture and resources available are appropriate to support the learning activity.

Left
Spaces around a learning hub.
Caulfield Grammar School,
Victoria, Australia

DESIGNING FOR THE TRANSITION TO SECONDARY AND BEYOND

The Caulfield facility was designed around the concepts of collaboration, diversity, democracy and negotiation. Learning activities have been grouped together to provide working spaces for a learning community of up to 93 students and six staff. There are four distinct zones: Launch Pad, Collaborative Studio, Workshop and Hub, containing up to 33 unique and purposeful settings, each created with bespoke resources, furniture and technology supporting a particular learning activity.

But does it work?

For the Caulfield project it was acknowledged that the design of contemporary learning spaces had to be driven by pedagogy. But does it work?

Quoting the staff, the outcomes and the lessons from the first few years of its operation are salutary:

> 'Students are flexible beings and we find they adapt very quickly (much quicker than adults) to a new environment.'

> 'Very quickly we see students moving from the position of taking a "back seat" and sitting at a desk with their hand in the air, to students who know that to learn they must seek. The building provides the opportunity for them to be active; to have a go, to collaborate with peers to find a solution, to move to the next space to seek perspectives, to actively seek out the teacher.'

> 'This develops an active learner who knows what to do "next". It develops the student agency.'

> 'The children have become responsible, self-driven, independent and open-minded learners.'

> 'They are acutely aware that with choice comes responsibility. We design learning experiences that challenge, are open-ended, but have built-in accountability features that make use of technology to ensure learning outcomes are met.'

> 'Their ability to work collaboratively rather than merely cooperatively has been a fascinating change. Having the spaces to enable children to discuss, debate, challenge, reassess and formulate new ideas is very powerful.'

These are indeed powerful lessons. They show that change can happen and that behaviours, not spaces, are enclosed by architecture – and can positively promote new behaviours around learning. The design of contemporary learning spaces is driven by pedagogy and can make a very significant contribution in supporting and promoting the design of new learning landscapes.

PRIMARY LIBRARIES

Changing teaching methods and constant digital access mean discrete library spaces could become a thing of the past – or remain a treasured destination in the school

Libraries have always played a role in developing more personalized approaches to learning. In primary schools they have provided creative and stimulating environments to explore, learn and engage with all types of books, media and artefacts.

In early years and primary environments, the planning of library and resource spaces needs to be considered in line with the pedagogy and desired organization of learning spaces. In collaborative or shared spaces and open learning landscapes, a more dispersed model for the location of resources and quieter reading areas may be developed rather than a single, centralized library. Enclosed or semi-enclosed spaces for small or class groups, suitable for group storytelling, individual reading and role play, are now much easier to incorporate.

It is important to consider if a discrete, dedicated library space for younger learners is necessary; and if it is, how might it be used as a shared and central resource for the school? The rationale for a more central space to house and store books and printed information needs to be reviewed in the light of pupils and staff having digital access to information throughout the school.

Because of this, some libraries for younger pupils are being repurposed as playful social spaces to focus more specifically on the role of story and fiction in early learning. This is enabled by the redistribution of non-fiction materials elsewhere throughout the school environment, freeing up space for platforms and dens to stimulate role play and oral storytelling. The ability of a library space to act as a vibrant place to stimulate the imagination must not be underestimated.

Access to a quiet space for personal reading in an environment with more choice over how to relax, read and access other resources has value for younger learners. A space that teachers can use for group work, guided reading activities, role play and presentations is also useful.

A primary school library is a space that can be curated by teachers or librarians to change its theme or focus according to the needs of the curriculum. In this way, it could provide information about the history and culture of the local environment, or support projects elsewhere in the school. The library should be a space that is easily reconfigurable for display and use.

As the importance of more applied, project-based learning grows within primary schools, library spaces are being augmented with maker-style spaces for collaborative project work activity.

Opposite above
A playful environment structured to prioritize storytelling and group reading. Stephen Perse Foundation Junior School, Cambridge, UK

Opposite below
Book storage and seating in a colourful, fun environment. Children's Library Billund, Billund, Denmark

CONSIDERATIONS

- A library space can be a special environment that inspires creativity and curiosity and is a fun place to learn.

- A library can be a defined space to promote group and individualized learning with support staff.

- An appropriate range of seating and furniture that can be easily reconfigured should be available.

- Books and resource materials should be displayed effectively and stored for ease of use and access.

- Surveillance and curation of books and artefacts may require a librarian role.

- Acoustic design and good levels of light are important.

SECONDARY LIBRARIES

Some argue that technology has rendered paper books obsolete, but libraries themselves are actually more relevant than ever

Opposite
Connected learning spaces.
The Gardens School, Auckland,
New Zealand

CONSIDERATIONS

- Finishes and lighting need to be robust and inviting. Lighting can imply areas of focus.

- A range of places with different characters means that pupils can find somewhere to gather in social groups, or for quiet individual study, supported by good acoustic design.

- The role of a librarian, and how information is stored and retrieved.

- The integration of digital and audio-visual equipment.

- Flexibility of furniture and how it can be configured for individuals or groups of different sizes.

- Provision of larger-scale presentations and exhibition spaces.

- The library should ideally be centrally located, close to primary circulation routes, with good visual connections both to these routes and to the external landscape.

In secondary education, the role of the library has been slowly changing in line with changing pedagogy, the reorganization of learning and the use of technology to access a wider and greater range of learning resources.

Libraries have always had a key role to play in gathering, researching and sharing knowledge between individuals and communities at a local, national and international level. They have been quick to respond to the changing demands for knowledge-transfer in secondary education and were early adopters of new technologies to access data and information within library facilities.

Debates have focused on the reduction in the use of books for reference and information-gathering. There is even an argument that the rapidly increasing use of new technologies renders obsolete the use of paper to experience and transfer knowledge. Statements about 'bookless' libraries abound and therefore, by implication, are libraries needed as special spaces within secondary schools at all?

It is now more important than ever to redefine the role of the library within the context of each school and its local community as it leads the transition to twenty-first century learning. The library is a resource hub for learning, and through its spaces, resources and the professional support of library staff, it still has a role to play in the school and local context.

Books are important things to explore and they are a useful method of selecting material for individual and group work. The visual connection that drives someone to pick up a book, explore it and discuss it with others, in a place that is comfortable and relaxed, is important. Libraries as learning and study areas that are always available for personal and small-group extended learning are needed more than ever. The use of new media technologies requires the rethinking of larger internal library spaces to create learning zones with more appropriate acoustic treatment to support new ways of learning.

The library as a resource hub for the developing school curriculum is important for both students and staff professional learning. The movement towards more research-based and applied learning means students must be able to access guidance on securing good information and data that is authentic and appropriate for them to use.

The role of the library as a curator of knowledge and artefacts, and a place to display past and future projects within the school, creates a future legacy. The library is a community resource that can be shared and can engage with both students and adults who may have special learning needs and whose main point of contact may be the library.

Libraries, by their nature, reach out and share information. They can establish new links with new content providers, and make virtual and real connections with higher education and commercial, business and social enterprise partners.

DESIGNING FOR COMMUNITY USE AND ENGAGEMENT

Schools must be designed so they can engage and interact with their communities, while still ensuring the safety of pupils and staff

A school is not an educating island; it is part of the community, so should be used by the community. The importance of family and community engagement is well established. To achieve this, the vision, culture and leadership of the school must make explicit that the school is open, interactive, engaging and communicative, rather than closed, remote and inaccessible.

In the earlier section 'How to begin', we stressed the importance of all stakeholders taking a collaborative approach in determining the vision for the school within its learning community and playing their part in putting it into practice.

Schools, at all phases of education, are now deciding for whom they are designing their spaces. In the shift to more student-centred approaches, learners as well as staff are co-designers of the spaces for their learning activities. Consideration needs to be given to the potential use of these spaces outside of current traditional school hours. But it's also important to think how parents and members of the community might interact with the school and support learning in a safe and secure way during the normal day. Many schools may not have the resources to develop exploratory design studios and maker spaces for younger learners, but they may be achievable in partnership with business, commercial and community providers, on the premises or off-site. This is particularly true with programmes of applied and vocational learning for older students.

Safety, security and safeguarding arrangements will always need to be of the highest priority because of increasing concerns over incidents of injury and violence in schools. Many architects, school leaders and communities are working together to ensure innovatory and dynamic learning spaces can be designed without the school appearing to be a fortress within its community. Building community is not just about shared space but ensuring that inclusive approaches are in place to be able to respond equally to all interests, cultures and social groups. However, this fundamental aspect must be addressed through the initial design, organization and function of the building.

Opposite
Shared community and school
resource. Discovery Elementary
School, Arlington, VA, USA

Overleaf
Greensward Academy,
Hockley, UK

Specialist Spaces

HOW TO APPROACH SPECIALIST SPACES

Designing spaces for subjects such as science and design technology can throw up different challenges and opportunities as schools develop a different approach to learning and teaching

A new pedagogy is emerging with the emphasis on following a meaningful and relevant curriculum in a practical rather than theoretical way, studying actively rather than passively.

Across the school curriculum generally (and across all phases) this has led to a rethinking of the size, variety and connected nature of learning spaces and environments. The importance of developing multi-disciplinary approaches and integrated programmes of study in humanities and the liberal arts has been well established. This has led to high levels of creativity and innovation in the design, clustering and location of these spaces, their ability to be adaptable on a day-to-day basis and also their ability to change over time.

In science, design technology and other related areas of the curriculum that are seen as more specialist, a range of approaches has been established linked to the content, organization and delivery of the subjects in the school. The need will always exist for dedicated specialist facilities that demand high levels of investment and servicing to deliver some of these courses. Many of these spaces will require a detailed level of specification and be subject to important protocols for their use so that they meet appropriate health and safety regulations. This has resulted in innovative designs to ensure that the highly specialized nature of the curriculum can be delivered while at the same time providing learning spaces for design, enquiry, exploration and research. This has often been complemented by more lightly serviced and highly adaptable studio spaces that can provide active and multi-disciplinary approaches to applied and project-based learning.

Open and larger workshop-style spaces are being designed that can accommodate a wider range of practical activities and provide space for large-scale project work. Major trends in the grouping of specialist subjects with related subject areas have been well established through curriculum groupings such as STEM (Science, Technology, Engineering and Maths). The larger, warehouse-style approach to creating spaces – for specialist subjects, multi-disciplinary project activity and work-related study – enables the use and function of these spaces to change over time. When designing the space, how it is organized and where it is positioned on campus, it is also important to consider how it will connect with the outside, to enable connections with continuing educational, commercial and business opportunities and partnership between the school and other providers.

Opposite
Food technology through a kitchen lab. Carter G. Woodson School, Virginia, USA

SCIENCE LABORATORIES AND PREPARATION ROOMS

Architects and designers have a huge number of practicalities to consider when creating science laboratories for modern learning

The distinctive part of science education is the use of experimental work to enable learning and to engage students. At senior school level this requires laboratories, preparation areas and specialist stores. Science education also involves other learning styles; for example, individual study, group discussions, presentations and direct teaching. Providing separate spaces for these other styles can lead to exciting and motivating designs for the science suite.

Providing separate spaces does, however, require a whole-school vision that organizes time slots for science that are far longer than usual, along with team teaching and high levels of day-to-day organization. In practice, capital costs are higher but better learning outcomes and higher staff morale can result.

The traditional provision of one laboratory per class is far easier to timetable, but may require larger room sizes to accommodate the whole range of learning types. It is possible to develop traditional provision by including some other spaces alongside laboratories – for example, an area for individual study.

The production of smoke, fumes and excess heat is a normal part of science demonstrations and experiments. Fume extraction and assured ventilation are a vital part of the design of science areas (see Considerations, page 71).

Whole-school systems for the management of fire, safety, ventilation, heating and lighting will require modification for science areas. Some smoke or heat detectors will be activated by normal science experiments so they should be capable of being switched off for short periods; sprinkler systems likewise.

Energy-saving lighting systems based on movement can be dangerous in preparation rooms with technicians working at a bench for long periods. Interior chemical stores should have no direct heating inside.

Opposite
Innovation and colour in specialist spaces.
TH School, Vietnam

A science learning zone

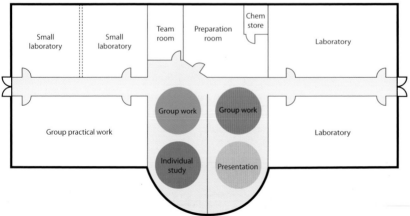

Small laboratory

Small laboratory

Team room

Preparation room

Chem store

Laboratory

Group practical work

Group work

Group work

Laboratory

Individual study

Presentation

SCIENCE LABORATORIES AND PREPARATION ROOMS

Each laboratory and preparation area requires gas, electricity, water and drainage services. They require individual master controls in each room.

The image presented is important. Bright, colourful, well-made furniture of innovative design appeals to students across the range of gender and ethnicity. Dull, old-fashioned wooden or black-topped benches create a fusty image for teachers and students.

Generally, benches are 800mm (31.5 inches) high, but student heights are increasing and 900mm (35.5 inches) is increasingly being used. This allows students to sit while writing but stand while doing experiments. Height-adjustable chairs that can be pushed under the benches during practical work are one solution.

The chairs should have backrests for ergonomic reasons, and skids or wide feet to ensure that they do not damage the floor. The floor itself should be non-slip and waterproof. It can match or contrast with the main colour scheme.

Information technology should be fully integrated and include display projection. Reflective, light-stop blinds (in light colours) should be installed to stop direct sunlight and provide the dim-out required for some experiments. Blackout is generally not required and can cause overheating by transmission of infra-red.

Moveable benches can be heavy to move and liable to damage fixed services where these are installed in the floor. Fixed benches and good design can mean easier and quieter movement for students when required. Alternatively, benches/tables can be free to move (opposite, below) if services are provided from an overhead system (opposite, above). Overhead systems help to future-proof science provision because they're easier to adapt or replace to provide additional services as science curricula develop.

Prep rooms

Laboratories cannot function without support spaces. Preparation rooms, with storage areas for equipment and materials, should be situated central to laboratories with floor area at the approximate ratio of one laboratory-equivalent space to every six laboratories. A ducted fume cupboard is essential, as are wet and dry preparation benches and good-sized washing-up areas. A coordinated tray storage system and racking make the most of space. Generic cupboards should be avoided as they are inefficient. Trolleys that are compatible with the trays make the movement of equipment easier.

A secure chemicals storeroom should open off the prep room and have ducted fume extraction as standard. The preferred location is north-facing (in the northern hemisphere) to avoid solar gain.

A team room should be provided for teachers and technicians to ensure that learning and preparation spaces are not taken over by administrative activities. This should be situated alongside the preparation room, although separate from it (see the sample design on the previous page).

Opposite above
Technology and overhead systems.

Opposite below
Adaptable tables around minimal fixed surfaces.
Dulwich College, London, UK

CONSIDERATIONS – VENTILATION

- Placing science rooms on the top floor reduces costs.

- Extract ducting from chemical store rooms and fume cupboards should terminate at stacks at least 1 metre (39 inches) above roof level and look much better if designed in.

- Ducting runs have to avoid structural building components.

- Boost ventilation should be integral and windows should be openable.

- Replacement air is important, so doors should not be too tight-fitting, or they may need grilles built in.

- Air-management systems should not cross-connect between rooms or corridors.

CONSIDERATIONS – CHECK POINTS

- Filter (recirculatory) fume cupboards or hoods are forbidden in most countries. They are inadvisable even where legally permitted because filters can only cover a restricted chemical spectrum and require regular (expensive) filter exchange. No filter can account for the range of current or future experiments, nor can it protect teachers with little expert knowledge of filter operation.

- Control of the gas supply is usually mandatory and is good practice in any case. Each room should have a central control valve system which checks for build-up of pressure and automatically cuts off supply if there are leaks.

- Check locally if water supplies to science areas are required to have systems fitted that prevent back-flow contamination of drinking water.

- Establish whether it is permitted to put chemical waste down the drains, or alternative disposal is required.

STEM, MAKER AND STUDIO SPACES

The spaces provided for hands-on and creative learning in science, technology, engineering and maths can have an impact across the whole curriculum and campus

The development of STEM programmes in schools enables students to learn about science, technology, engineering and mathematics by bringing these subjects together in the curriculum. The approach to learning is project-based, dealing with real-world issues within a social, economic and environmental context. The programmes promote a 'hands-on' creative approach to encourage students to design, experiment and test out their own solutions.

The development of STEM in the USA has led to art being included to create the more holistic STEAM as a curriculum area of study. In many countries, creativity is just assumed as a central aspect of project-based STEM activity.

The developing pedagogy for STEM and STEAM is leading to a 'maker' culture and the rethinking of learning spaces, labs and studio spaces. The academic Seymour Papert made eight assumptions about what 'maker' spaces in schools needed to achieve to enable a twenty-first century learning experience:

1. Learning by doing.

2. Technology as a building material.

3. Having fun.

4. Learning to learn.

5. Taking time.

6. You can't get it right without getting it wrong.

7. Do unto us what we do unto our students.

8. The digital world.

Consideration must be given to how to offer this experience at different ages. In elementary and primary schools a hands-on creative experience, using a range of materials to test, tinker, explore and build, will be important.

There must be a balance between low- and high-tech activity, and everyday materials, as well as commercial products such as Lego, Makeblock and many others, need to be freely available to stimulate learning further. As learners progress through primary and middle school, these approaches continue but the focus will be on the ability to solve real-world problems with a strong emphasis on teamwork and collaboration. At the secondary phase, the need to deliver the appropriate curriculum for each school will determine the range of equipment and facilities required.

Above
Large creative studio spaces for STEM and design technology. Royal Greenwich University Technical College, London, UK

CONSIDERATIONS

- Determine the organization's strategic curriculum approach to STEM/STEAM and other specialist subjects.

- Research and define the pedagogy and the range of learning activities and outcomes that your approach to STEM/STEAM will enable.

- Consider the range of labs and studio spaces that may need to be clustered together to support a STEM/STEAM curriculum-delivery model.

- Is the configuration of the learning space, equipment and furniture compatible with the intended approach to STEM/STEAM?

- In what ways can maker spaces enhance and support all areas of the curriculum?

- What role can the design and location of maker spaces play in extending and enriching the curriculum experience at pre-school and early years level?

- Consider the remodelling and refurbishment of existing spaces alongside any new building programmes.

ART

When designing a creative art space and deciding where to locate it, think about how art fits in with the rest of the curriculum

We have already identified the trend in many countries to place art as a subject discipline into STEM to create STEAM, a relevant and integrated project-based approach to learning. Although welcome at face value, this approach risks including art as a subject silo rather than a core pedagogy – as if the creative arts were something you might do on a Tuesday afternoon, rather than something that may prove intrinsic to all learning for young people. Either way, the physical, technical and environmental dimensions are critical to the success of the learning space. An arts education programme will make an essential contribution to any agenda for twenty-first century learning and teaching. It will motivate, engage, enrich and improve outcomes for all learners, and especially those who at times can be hard to reach.

An arts programme within schools will offer a range of experiences (visual arts, design, sculpture, pottery, creative materials and textile design) through strong links with digital media, technology, music and performance.

The pedagogy and the intended organization of learning within schools need to be well defined in order to create an appropriate design. Art studios, art barns and design centres are all associated with specialist functions and activities.

The importance of display, research and discussion of work is essential in art studios, as is the opportunity to display completed work to a wider audience. There is great motivation and personal reward in the public recognition of work. As in all enquiry- and project-based approaches, showing work in progress and illustrating the end products is an essential part of the design process.

It is important to consider what takes place in art studios, how it connects to other curriculum areas, and how this will influence the design and positioning of new art spaces. Plymouth School of Creative Arts, also known as The Red House, is a mainstream city-centre school in the UK for three to sixteen year-olds in which the approach to learning in all subjects adopts a traditional art school ethos of learning-through-making. This means a learning culture whose natural habitat is the studio and the workshop, and movement between both inside and outside.

There is continual traffic between The Red House, Plymouth College of Art's pre-degree campus, and the specialist workshop environments at the College's higher education campus. The College was also a founding member of Tate Exchange in London, and the School and College occupy the fifth floor of Tate Modern's Blavatnik Building for a week each year.

Opposite
Glass blowing within creative art. Plymouth College of Arts, Plymouth, UK

MUSIC AND PERFORMANCE

....

When considering spaces for the performing arts within schools it is important to take account of the vision and culture for learning in the school and the community, the pedagogy and the internal organization of the subjects

High levels of creative activity in the school curriculum, especially those related to multi-disciplinary and project-based approaches, require a wider variety and location of studio-style spaces in which such activities can be conducted. A school with a strong focus on the performing arts may want those facilities to be highly visible within the school and to demonstrate this to the wider school community. In developing a strong specialism within the performing arts, where extensive and regular theatrical productions will be staged, external partnerships with other providers and community groups need to be considered.

It is important that spaces for theatre, dance, drama and music are adequately designed and fitted out to meet the required performance needs and standards. Drama studios need the capacity to be a black box and closed to adjacent spaces so that the appropriate atmosphere and mood can be created. Lighting and sound systems are important and therefore appropriate acoustic treatments need to be in place. Drama studios require ample floor area and specifications will vary from country to country. A good guide for class-size groups is at least 120–150 square metres (1,292–1,615 square feet) to include an area for performance of approximately 90 square metres (969 square feet). The height of the studio needs to be at least 4.3 metres (14 feet) to ensure the appropriate angles of lighting can be achieved and that staging can be introduced. The size of such spaces needs further consideration for audience participation – for example, by using high-quality screens and folding walls an adjacent space to the drama studio can be created for a small amount of audience seating.

Dance studios require a high person-to-space ratio of at least 5 square metres (54 square feet) per person and require high ceilings for dance and assessment activities. A sprung floor is always the preferred option and the shape of the space must ensure appropriate mirror provision for the size of the intended groups. Sound and media provision are standard in such spaces and good acoustic treatment is important. Music and drama activities may need individual and group room support to deliver the curriculum, as well as adequate access to changing/ green room facilities during rehearsals and productions.

Above
Adaptable spaces for drama and dance. Trumpington Community College, Cambridge, UK

CONSIDERATIONS

- Specialist performance facilities are best grouped together for cross-curriculum support and the need for good acoustic treatment.

- Adaptable and well-designed adjacent social and gathering spaces can make performance visible within the school and more easily accessible for community use and productions.

- Campus and site location needs consideration if these specialist facilities need to be easily accessible for community use.

- The co-location of art and design technology studios and maker spaces will improve the ability of all students to support and prepare materials, sets, props and media for performance events.

- Multi-functional performing arts spaces will need to consider flexible acoustic treatments: drama requires different reverberation times to music, for instance.

TECHNOLOGY AND COMMUNICATIONS

The use of digital technology – now a fundamental aspect of modern learning environments – can bring engagement and enjoyment to learning. It can also offer new challenges and opportunities

When digital technologies first emerged, they were expensive and schools often became the hubs for innovation. In many communities, the internet was first available within the context of an educational environment, whether that was the local school library, further education (FE) college or university. At that time, technology dictated the organization of rooms and departments. Furniture was 'device specific' and nearly always static. The spaces often prohibited learning by placing the emphasis on the integration of the technology above the needs of the learner. But a learning space needs to be enabled by technology, not driven by it, and this static approach is redundant. Technology is now mobile, flexible and cheap. Today's devices, whether carried in a pocket or worn around a wrist, are infinitely more powerful than the hardware used to send mankind to the moon in the 1960s.

Digital technology now permeates everything we do and dominates the world of work. It is not unreasonable, therefore, to expect school design to adapt to this changing world and make the most of opportunities this technology offers.

How should this be approached?
When considering how best to design for technology integration, planners need to think beyond the hardware that is currently available. They need to anticipate that the use and application of technology will naturally be integrated into every aspect of a new learning space. This means integrating systems and structures for learning and teaching, leadership, management and administration.

This is not about being brave and innovative as designers, it's about replicating the real world and embracing the 'now' over the traditional forms of space, pedagogy and culture. Looking at a technology-enabled learning space should not start with the technology, it should start with the pedagogy and culture.

Infrastructure

Getting the infrastructure right in a learning space is a strong foundation for success. Designers need to ask:

- Has the infrastructure been designed to support the multiple personal devices that might be used?

- Is there sufficient connectivity?

- Is the active network infrastructure configured to support the data that needs to be processed?

- Is the wireless infrastructure designed to support the device strategy?

- Are there adequate online safety controls and protocols?

To future-proof our schools, planners need to make sure their power and data infrastructure is universal. If budget is constrained, designers should focus on the power requirements first, because data-software networks can always be added wirelessly later.

Planners should ask themselves how learners will be able to use digital technology flexibly across the learning space. Outdoor spaces must be included in the plans. Different layouts and a range of pedagogical approaches should be considered. Both educators and, most importantly, the learners should be engaged in the process. How might their requirements change?

When working on a project that is institution-wide, designers should envisage the use of technologies, including display technologies, in all learning and teaching areas. In addition, consider judicious use of technology in public areas and circulation spaces. Anticipate that as a learning community grows, every space has the potential to be a 'learning space'.

Above (both)
Integrating paper and screen.
West Thornton Primary
Academy, London, UK

TECHNOLOGY AND COMMUNICATIONS

Devices

No single device can fulfil every learning need. Therefore schools must prepare their learners for this by embedding a range of devices into every learning space. Students will need to be competent on multiple platforms, operating systems and interfaces. Our learning spaces must be designed to prepare them to be more versatile and adaptive than ever before.

Furniture

The selection of furniture should enable the integration of technology to support learning. Choices should promote learners working comfortably and ergonomically. This should be the case on an individual, partner or group basis and may involve moveable lap trays or sliding tables to support devices. Sufficient space and easy access to relevant power and peripherals are essential. Learners should be able to use any specialist devices safely and readily.

Mechanical and electrical

The provision of heating, lighting and sound must meet the needs of all learning. Internal design must ensure 'lines of sight' are good across the learning space, it must be well ventilated and heated, and sound must be equalized, too.

REWARDS:

Advances in technology support a more flexible and agile approach to technology-enabled learning.

RISKS:

Overdominance of one commercial partner can lead to a school operating a one-device or one-operating-system specific approach.

It's all about learning – not technology

When planning learning spaces, recognize the difference between the technology that is required to run the back-office systems and the technology that is applied to the learning and teaching process. Technology is integral to high-quality support systems such as HR (human resources), payroll, email, communication systems, data tracking, monitoring and analysis. All of these improve outcomes.

Planners should avoid individual preferences for a particular technology. Instead, in collaboration with stakeholders, designers should evaluate and share the effectiveness of technologies on a wide range of activities and outcomes.

Consider how and why stakeholders will use the technology *before* considering what technology should be integrated. Learning, rather than technology, should drive change.

Opposite
Design for a variety of learning devices and equipment

ARTIFICIAL INTELLIGENCE

The introduction of artificial intelligence (AI) will have a profound effect not only on pupils' learning outcomes, but also on the classroom itself

It's not easy to peer into the future but the mists are beginning to clear. Conventional technology has so far been used to improve school administration, but within the classroom its use has been limited. The blackboard has become a whiteboard with added interactivity, yet with no improved educational outcomes. However, the introduction of blended learning, mixing the online with the offline, is beginning to show better results.

This will improve dramatically with the introduction of AI. In his book *The Fourth Education Revolution*, Sir Anthony Seldon, the vice-chancellor of the University of Buckingham, predicts that AI will have the power to make a real difference to pupil performance. Schools will be able to manage all pupil data and ensure that all academic work is always pitched at exactly the right level, leading directly to improved learning outcomes.

Sir Anthony also predicts that 'separate classrooms will disappear in time and be replaced by pods and wide-open flexible spaces that can be configured for individual and flexible collective learning. Sensors will monitor individual students, picking up on their changes faster and more accurately than any teacher could.'

And it's not just within the learning environment that artificial intelligence will be used. Personalized acoustics, lighting, temperature and even seating position will be possible. The integration of AI into school furniture, taking advantage of the Industrial Internet of Things (IIOT), means that each chair will become a personal chair.

Michael B. Horn, the co-founder of the Clayton Christensen Institute, whose mission is 'improving the world through disruptive innovation', has described the future classroom as a 'learning studio' where 'spaces are built for different activities which can occur individually through digital media or in small interactive groups'. He argues that schools 'won't have conventional classrooms and each student will begin their day with just their personal workplan'.

Opposite above
Enriching the personal learning experience

Opposite below
DIY collaborative hubs

CONSIDERATIONS

- Schools may have to provide extra services – from counselling and mentoring to health services and free meals – and will need the spaces required to support them.

- Dedicated space will always be needed for physical activity and the arts.

- Schools could become smaller in size and more rooted in the community.

MEDIA

....

The world of media is changing faster than we can build. How do we plan for this?

Planners should expect ongoing shake-ups in media in the near future and should be mindful of the rate and speed of change when working with a client.

While many specialisms no longer require specific spaces, your client may request specific suites for activities such as:

- Videography.

- Virtual reality.

- Photography.

- Animation.

- Augmented reality.

- Music technology.

- Computer science.

If working on a traditional flat-based network infrastructure, designers may want to consider co-locating media space provision near the main server room or close to technical support services. Spaces to break out and work on elements of a project without the assistance of technology can also be useful. Planners may wish to consider co-location with a library or learning commons to provide flexibility and capacity.

Designers should be mindful when designing specific spaces for a media specialism that requirements *will* change over time. Any space should have the flexibility to grow, adapt and change as required. Planners are therefore encouraged to avoid fixed storage or display units or hardware-specific furniture, fixtures and equipment (FF&E) solutions.

Far too many schools fall into the trap of their media suite becoming a 'statement space' where the latest technology or trend is showcased to entice potential applicants but where very little impact is made on learning. These spaces often become tired over time and become the white elephant that a school cannot afford to upgrade or replace. Designers should consider how the media space will work when the static technology installed becomes obsolete.

Opposite
Modern media spaces need to be open and flexible

CONSIDERATIONS:
- Specialist spaces provide a focal point for expert resources and input.

- Specialism becomes confined to the space and does not penetrate the wider curriculum-delivery or learner experience.

- Spaces can become dated quickly as the rate and speed of change and disruption in this field is rapid.

APPLIED AND TECHNICAL LEARNING

Applied and technical learning in schools is leading to new strategies and design approaches for the school and college curriculum

Students are being introduced at ever-younger ages to more relevant and authentic learning scenarios that combine passive and active instruction. As early as primary and middle school, students are gaining knowledge and understanding of career paths and the opportunities that are in front of them. As students develop their interests and passions, these multi-disciplinary and project-based approaches support more informed decision-making. At the heart of this, students are presented with 'real life' challenges in problem-solving, design and innovation. These challenges help to develop the critical thinking and collaborative skills needed to improve their approach to learning and to prepare them for life and work.

In the United Kingdom, university technical colleges (UTCs) have been established to deliver technical education, as well as core curriculum subjects, for fourteen to nineteen year-olds. In Finland, recent new approaches have been developed to deliver vocational qualifications and the 'skills for life' within the school system. In the USA, Career and Technical Education (CTE) came into prominence to fill the gap between high school and post-secondary pursuits.

Maker spaces: applied and vocational learning

Maker spaces have grown in popularity as a response to the need for more engaging and real-world learning opportunities for students. The maker culture breaks down into three phases: pre-making, making and post-making. In the pre-making phase, students are developing a wide range of skills that include:

- Project and time management.

- Mentoring and coaching with internal or external leaders.

- Planning, research and even rapid-prototyping.

As the prototyping leads to the production of the actual project, students transition into the making phase. This allows students to learn about:

- Production sequencing and scheduling.

- The variety of equipment needed to make their unique product.

Opposite
Hands-on repair. Gene A.
Buinger Career and Technical
Education Academy in Bedford,
Texas, USA

APPLIED AND TECHNICAL LEARNING

Once the final project is complete, the post-making phase provides opportunities to:

- Present both their process and project to an audience of students and/or leaders.

- Defend the design or methodologies to a panel of educators responsible for assessing and evaluating the students' learning.

While maker spaces are space and equipment intensive, the making phase – and indeed the entire maker culture – provides rich opportunities for students to develop the skills they will need to be successful.

Many of the projects embarked upon by students in CTE courses follow a similar model to the maker culture. High school students have multiple opportunities to benefit from the three phases of the maker culture when enrolling in CTE courses, but the foundation skills can be developed much earlier in the school career. Many elementary schools are focused on providing maker spaces either as stand-alone spaces or integrated into libraries. Many schools are developing a maker culture by developing programmes of study that integrate appropriate subjects and skills for learning into a singular course of study or project.

At its core, a vocational, technical and career curriculum is experiential and hands-on. The labs and studios are designed for active learning, which complements more passive learning methods. In science disciplines, students research and explore theories and concepts in the classroom before moving to a lab to test them. In this environment students are at the centre of their learning and are immersed not just in the content but more importantly in the process.

The design of labs and studio spaces needs to model an approach that:

- Provides the space and tools for students to lead learning.

- Reinforces and builds upon concepts they've previously learned.

- Utilizes a variety of technology and specialized equipment to complete the work.

At an advanced level, the design of these labs draws upon professional environments. Furniture, technology and access to materials are used to immerse students in a real-world environment. Space is transformed to establish relevant training grounds, from professional-grade culinary kitchens, automotive technology shops and fabrication labs to courtrooms, smart hospitals and robotics arenas. This approach provides students with opportunities to explore careers without commitment or fear of failure.

For many students in the USA, the CTE classes provide a way to pursue careers directly following graduation or that act as a foundation for higher-level certification programmes.

Health science fields serve as an excellent example. The medical field is vast and employs personnel with a range of certifications and degree levels. At the Ben Barber Innovation Academy in Mansfield, Texas, students can earn certification as a Certified Nursing Assistant, Pharmacy Technician, Insurance Coding Specialist or Medical Technician. They participate in clinical rotations and internships and have a 'living' hospital at their school.

Opposite above
Georgetown High School's new career and technology labs are designed as autonomous spaces. Georgetown High School, Texas, USA

Opposite below
Making project-based learning explicit in studio spaces. High-Tech High, San Diego, California, USA

APPLIED AND TECHNICAL LEARNING

Design considerations

There are a number of key considerations of design when developing spaces for vocational, career and technical education. Design parameters such as locally adopted codes, appropriate spatial adjacencies and connections to other commercial activities are important. The modular construction of facilities is important to maximize efficiency and allow for easy reconfiguration of space, because vocational needs and processes demands change over time.

Many programmes are universal and simply need a large floor space and access to utilities, while others have space requirements that need to adapt to more equipment and a higher level of infrastructure. For example:

- Cosmetology frequently requires numerous stations (hair-washing, hair-dressing, manicure and pedicure), many of which demand constant access to water. Additionally, storage is needed for the tools, materials and mannequins that are required to fully prepare students for certification.

- Auto shops that include vehicle lifts are space intensive and require tool, chemical and equipment storage as well as sufficient space for the total number of lifts needed.

- Culinary arts programmes are centred around commercial kitchen layouts and often include dining and instructional areas as well as dry storage, coolers and freezers.

Building codes specify requirements for fire protection and emergency evacuation similar to those applying to large shop spaces that house hazardous equipment and/or chemicals.

Since their inception, American CTE programmes have responded to workforce and economic demands in the private sector. Many school systems collaborate with the larger community when designing vocational campuses or evolving existing programmes. Local business owners can be valued partners in the selection and development of CTE programmes and course offerings. Many are willing to serve as guest lecturers, while others donate equipment and resources.

Key questions

There are three important discussion themes to consider when planning and designing spaces:

- Ownership of space.
- Location within a building or campus.
- The role of student recruitment into programmes.

These are questions that will inform, define or refine the campus and programme culture.

Above
This space can be reconfigured easily for other activities. Gene A. Buinger Career and Technical Education Academy in Bedford, Texas, USA

Ownership of space: What level of ownership is appropriate for instructional and shop spaces? A campus or programme culture that centres around educator teams and collaboration may lead to the sharing of space, students and time. If spaces are shared by educators, it is necessary to plan and design for complementary administrative space.

Location: What role does CTE play in campus or system branding, and how should the location of vocational educational spaces support that role? If vocational education is a focal point for a campus, then these spaces may be wanted at the front and centre, with the students, programmes and projects visible. In addition, if vocational learning programmes offer services to the public, the pathway for public travel must also be considered.

Student recruitment: Should students' work (in-progress or complete) serve as a recruiting tool for these programmes or courses? If so, the projects should be visible by the general student population, encourage students to inquire about programme enrolment and make positive engagement with providers. Many programmes are moving towards a focus on providing students with opportunities for exploration. This shift is part of a movement towards passion-based learning to achieve higher levels of engagement while students also learn about the wide array of career opportunities now available and that continue to grow and diversify.

A PLACE TO GATHER

Everywhere is a learning space

Many schools are eager to establish a specific place that is central to the school's design and organization – somewhere large that promotes informal and formal learning opportunities as the lifeblood that runs through the building: a 'heart' space, which strongly reflects the values, culture and approach to learning of the school. A 'heart' space can become a destination that encourages movement and flow to a central area that celebrates the work of the school within its local learning community.

These central areas need to work hard and provide a range of adjacent and connected spaces that promote the vision for learning and teaching that the school believes in. The choice of social, catering and ancillary functions in these larger gathering areas will be important. The location and access to the specialist facilities that support and enable performing arts productions and audience participation on a small or larger scale need to be considered. Many large, central 'heart' spaces, atria, or street and central mall spaces in schools have suffered from a lack of purpose and definition at the design stage. These spaces must be more than 'nice to have' and should provide a variety of choice as to where, when and how to learn as well as maximizing connections to related specialist studios and facilities.

Gathering spaces can form the cultural hub of the school, but also the wider community: these spaces could all be utilized by visiting speakers, local businesses, parents, clubs, other schools and so on. It is important therefore that the gathering space is easily accessible, inviting, reflective of the school community, and able to support many different types of use.

The acoustics, air flow and lighting within these larger spaces needs careful attention and must relate to the wide-ranging functionality of such spaces and patterns of occupancy. Where the building is readily accessible by the community, the safety and security of learners must also be addressed.

The size of a school and the age range of its students will determine the appropriateness of central 'heart' spaces. Both larger and smaller schools will wish to create gathering spaces in a more dispersed and diverse way. Collaborative spaces are an important design feature of any school, both for social learning and to promote cross-disciplinary activities and dialogue. Adjacent routeways can be made wider not only to improve circulation but also to create spaces to pause, meet and study. Gathering spaces can play a major role in enabling the work of the school to be put on display in the form of exhibitions, performances and large-scale projects.

Opposite
Learning in all spaces.
Hazel Wolf K-8, Seattle,
Washington, USA

CONSIDERATIONS

- Gathering spaces are multi-functional in nature and must respond to potential use.

- Larger gathering spaces need to be close to primary circulation routes.

- The degree of enclosure of larger gathering spaces needs consideration due to noise and movement.

- Fixed, stepped seating can be used to increase the audience capacity, and also acts as an informal learning area.

- Determine how frequently larger groups within the school will want to use the space.

- Sunken spaces within larger areas can form effective places for groups to congregate.

- Media and technology are needed to enhance the potential uses of gathering spaces.

- Support spaces such as chair stores or rooms for audio-visual equipment will be required.

- Can you create 'pop up' units and larger displays in your gathering spaces with access to drive in a vehicle for large-scale projects?

A PLACE FOR STAFF

Don't forget about the needs of staff when designing schools and other learning spaces – and it isn't just a question of 'do we need a staffroom?'

The shift to a more personalized and learner-centred approach, which puts the emphasis on engagement, means staff will be expected to work more collaboratively in their role as enablers of learning. As the pedagogy, curriculum and organization of learning changes, the design of more diverse and adaptable learning spaces will develop.

All learners need to feel they are valued, supported and have a sense of self-worth in these new environments; the same is true for all staff. Just as we need to determine the learning activities and environments that make this easier for learners, so too must the needs of staff be considered when creating new spaces.

As a professional learning community within a learning organization, the dialogue should not be reduced to 'do we need or not need a staffroom?'

The full range of elements that the staff need in order to support learners and develop, share and manage their own professional learning needs to be determined. There is a key strategic role for school leadership to ensure that this takes place and it needs to be applied to all aspects of life and work within the school.

Opposite above
Providing refreshment and relaxation for staff. Freemans Bay School, Auckland, New Zealand

Opposite below
Providing a collaborative space. Freemans Bay School, Auckland, New Zealand

CONSIDERATIONS

- What arrangements are in place to ensure that all staff's personal belongings are in a safe, secure but accessible space during their time at work? Don't forget to take account of outdoor equipment and the need to shower/change clothing.

- The location and accessibility of rest rooms, relaxation and quiet spaces; consider the size of the campus and timings/duration of learning sessions.

- Learning, year and phase spaces will require a range of appropriate places for staff to collaborate with their immediate colleagues over their planning, management and leadership of learning.

- Bearing in mind the school's protocols, consider space(s) for staff to store, prepare and consume their own food – particularly out of hours – and to accommodate specific dietary requirements.

- Areas where staff can come together as a whole school to meet and have dialogue, address whole-school strategic planning, share practice and experience, undertake training and development and study.

- Spaces that can be used for whole-community interactions.

PLACES FOR EXTERNAL LEARNING

It is widely recognized that outdoor learning can promote happier, healthier and more engaged and motivated students

We have already mentioned the importance of play and creative activity, and the important connections between inside and outside learning spaces. Many studies have shown that a more direct connection with nature can moderate cognitive fatigue and improve levels of concentration for all students, especially those with ADHD (attention deficit hyperactivity disorder). Extensive studies in the UK have concluded that learning outdoors will, as the Natural Connections Demonstration Project of 2016 puts it, 'deliver a range of positive outcomes for teachers and pupils'.

In addition to a range of research and publications that supports the way external environments improve creativity and imaginative play, the outdoor environment offers collaborative learning opportunities and at the same time it encourages learners to develop independence and autonomy. There is a wider international debate about re-engaging young people in the benefits of visiting large public and wild outdoor spaces to improve health and mental well-being.

In supporting the shift towards learning and teaching that is more personal for the learner, outside spaces need to be seen as equal in importance to those inside. External environments create opportunities for structured and unstructured play and can be designed to enable learners to experience risk and challenge.

The natural habitats surrounding schools are often under-utilized. The cycle of seasons and growth of plants, the sound of wind through trees, the patterns of light and shade and the experience of running water all enhance learning.

Opportunities exist in the external landscape to define group spaces, imaginative walks, physical challenges and larger amphitheatre arenas for class gatherings or performances. This can be achieved by the use of topography, surface differentiation, built-in equipment, screens, structures and inviting natural habitats.

Where external space is limited, ground-floor decking can create new levels on which to learn, and upper floors can have secure terraces. Ensure that what is usually done inside can also be done outside, by providing wireless connectivity across the school site. In addition, developing a range of strategies that bring nature and the outside into the day-to-day experience will further enhance learning.

Opposite above
A fully enclosed courtyard with playful furniture that allows different ways of gathering and performing. Stephen Perse Foundation Junior School, Cambridge, UK

Opposite below
Outdoor places for fun and creative play. Hazel Wolf K-8, Seattle, Washington, USA

CONSIDERATIONS

- Consider the operation of doors, thresholds and lines of security to facilitate easy pupil access to external spaces.

- The integration of a soft landscape, trees and plants can support biodiversity and form rich learning spaces that promote well-being.

- Provide covered spaces to protect learners and external resources

from the extremes of the local climate. These could be outdoor 'rooms' or canopies that form deep thresholds to internal spaces.

- Undulations in topography and the differentiation of surface materials can not only add visual interest but also define smaller learning zones within a wider learning landscape.

- Use external furniture to suggest patterns of use.

- Early years learning should allow direct connections to covered external learning spaces.

- Secondary students need access to external landscape facilities and habitats that link directly to their curricula.

- Develop learning partnerships with others in the community who are responsible for and develop natural habitats.

Bringing it Together

FLOW AND NAVIGATION

Rethink the way students use all of a building as we move from teacher-directed to student-centered learning

This environment should promote collaborative and multi-disciplinary work. Navigation routes and flow must be developed to support and encourage this connectivity. Approaching this design should be from the 'inside-out' – that is, designing from what teachers and students need to do and creating the appropriate environment in which to achieve this. There will be a need for a variety of differing learning spaces, perhaps clustered into connected learning zones.

The concept of movement within the school environment changes; every step along the way may create an opportunity for formal or informal learning. Circulation spaces can form a large part of the built area of a school, so it is important that these can act as positive spaces in their own right and add to the culture and learning of the school.

Learning environments need to be fluidly connected by space to promote navigation and flow of movement. The principal learning zones could be connected by interstitial 'nodes' that act as learning destinations and points of reference to aid wayfinding. Nodes may act as spaces in which to spend extended periods, or drop-in short-stay learning opportunities. Some may connect and form extensions to social destinations – for example, dining; some may provide gallery display or places for sharing community information. These nodal points do not need to be strictly defined as spaces; they can loosely connect adjacent learning environments, but alternatively they can be expressed with their own character and purpose.

Both horizontal and vertical circulation can become part of this 'field' of learning within the school. Staircases can be designed to open into and be part of spaces that suggest gathering or group activity. Areas below staircases can become 'cave'-type spaces for learning. All spaces for movement should be considered for their potential learning opportunity.

Opposite
A central hub connecting spaces and providing a wider range of learning opportunities. Stanley Park High School, London, UK

Previous page
The Vittra Telefonplan School, Stockholm, Sweden

CONSIDERATIONS

- Colour, lighting, graphics and display form a key part of the engagement of these spaces.

- Routeways can be widened at key points to allow the integration of alcoves, seating or other nodal spaces that can form areas suitable for resting, socializing or informal learning.

- Visual connections to external areas and primary learning spaces can aid wayfinding and add to the sense of activity and community of the school.

- Movement spaces should be designed to accommodate expected peak flows during normal activity in the school day, and also to act efficiently in the event of an emergency.

- Access to storage elements such as lockers and cloakrooms should be integrated into the design of circulation spaces without impinging on the clear widths required.

- The most appropriate furnishing and equipment needs to be identified and integrated as part of the initial design concept.

- Wayfinding and security must support and complement the ethos and approach to learning and teaching within the school campus.

HOW THE SPACES CAN COME TOGETHER

Schools are composed of many different learning spaces, as well as other supporting functions. We explore a number of concepts that bring the spaces together

We have established that an effective twenty-first century learning environment is the physical representation of a well-functioning learning culture in which values, beliefs and pedagogical practices are shared and experienced by everyone involved in the daily life and work of the school.

The move to a more student-centred approach to learning and teaching encourages and enables a more dynamic, creative and engaging learning experience that has more relevance and personal ownership for the learner. New learning zones with a greater variety of spaces and more emphasis on applied learning and multi-disciplinary activity will be developed. These approaches are developing from the early years through to secondary and continuing education.

Although the design of schools is dictated by many external factors, including the physical and legislative constraints of the site, the three examples that follow show different ways of bringing learning spaces together: an early years facility with external connections, a primary school with learning spaces arranged as class-bases in a 'family' grouping, and a secondary school with spaces arranged to form a supportive 'transition' zone for new-intake pupils.

Following the ideas established earlier in this book, each example consists of four areas:

1. Objectives: what does the school want to achieve with the new environment?

2. Crucial choices: what strategic decisions have been made to inform a design concept?

3. Learning spaces: what kinds of learning spaces best support the objectives and crucial choices?

4. Design solution: how can the benefits and opportunities of these decisions become a deliverable and communicable design?

Please note that there are many ways of arranging learning spaces that are driven by pedagogy and culture as much as any other factor. Additionally, funding streams can dictate the arrangement and size of spaces. Therefore there are numerous school designs: this chapter indicates theoretical examples specifically illustrating some of the ideas explained in previous chapters.

Opposite
Creating spaces in other places.
Dame Bradbury's School,
Saffron Walden, UK

EARLY YEARS

As part of a primary school extension, a new series of spaces was proposed to form a new 50-pupil nursery and pre-school over a single storey. Offering an extensive external learning programme, easy connections to the outdoors were important

An existing primary school highlighted a community need for the provision of a new 50-pupil nursery and pre-school for pupils aged two to four years. An area of the school grounds was identified for the extension, which was intended to support the 'Forest School' activities that will form a core of the pedagogy.

Contextual facts

- Primary school extension.
- 50-pupil nursery and pre-school.
- Not possible to link to existing infants' spaces.
- Extensive use of outdoor spaces.

Objectives

- Stimulate play and exploration: the space should allow controlled free movement of pupils between external and internal spaces, supported with stimulating and relevant resources.

- Promote active learning and creativity: the new facility should enable pupils to find and become embedded within tasks and activities they find absorbing, with spaces that can be quickly altered to lend support.

- Ensure safety and well-being: the spaces should promote connections to the outside, be open, ensure good visual surveillance and maintain security.

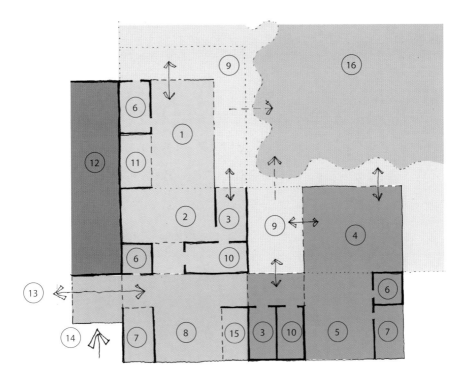

Crucial choices

KEY

1. Nursery active area
2. Nursery wet area
3. Cloakrooms
4. Pre-school active area
5. Pre-school wet area
6. Resources
7. Staff
8. Flexible communal space
9. External covered area
10. Toilets/changing
11. Nursery quiet space
12. Existing school
13. School connection
14. Pre-school access
15. Food prep
16. Landscape for external learning and play

- Location: it was not possible to link the new facility with the existing reception year of the school, so a decision was made to provide a dedicated access for pupil and parents that is away from the other existing school access points.

- Use: the facility is available for 30 two to three year-olds and 30 three to four year-olds throughout the day, with potential for half-day and after-school provision.

- Layout: it was decided to split the new facility into three primary internal learning spaces. These were dedicated to nursery and pre-school pupils, with a third communal space for shared use and learning.

- Appearance: to promote visual connections to the outside, the new spaces were provided with good levels of glazing and child-height window seats enabling views out at lower levels for children. Along with additional rooflights, the glazing admits excellent levels of daylight into the space and forms a strong connection to the external landscape from the internal spaces. Throughout the space, natural materials were used for internal finishes and fittings to enhance the well-being of staff and pupils.

EARLY YEARS

Learning spaces

The following types of learning space were considered to support the key objectives:

- Open wet/active zones within the nursery and pre-school learning space.

- Easily accessible and flexible communal space providing a space for group work as well as a parent space.

- A food prep area for snacktimes and lunch support.

- Toilets available for easy direct access from the external covered areas.

- Spacious resource stores to enable activities to be easily and swiftly curated by school staff.

Design solution

- The final design proposes two linked nursery and pre-school spaces with a communal space acting as a shared learning area between them, which provides a point of access for pupils and parents, as well as giving the wider school a space to use for larger gatherings.

- The spaces use cloakrooms as lobbies to the outside, and to enable changing into outdoor clothing. Because groups of pupils spend much time outdoors, toilets are easily accessible through these areas.

- Covered areas allow a seamless inside/outside flow of learning, forming a transitional threshold for the layout of resources and sheltered play. Glazed walls to the internal spaces can be opened up further to the outdoors under the control of school staff.

- The spaces are open-plan and supported by a combination of built-in fittings and loose furniture to enable a changing, flexible interior environment. Fittings such as sinks or interactive screens can become fixed points, with mobile trolleys, shelves and equipment designed to be able to 'dock' around these fixed elements, enabling different learning zones to be formed and reconfigured easily within the space. Walls with acoustic absorbing material can help to designate these zones, providing areas which are quieter and acoustically sheltered from more open learning spaces.

CONSIDERATIONS

- Ease of drop-offs for parents was a key consideration, so the position of cloakrooms needed to be easily accessible from the pupil entrance.

- As part of the school day, pupils spend much time outdoors and enjoying woodland environments. The cloakrooms had to provide adequate space and access for coats and muddy boots for small groups of pupils at a time.

- Often, parents require close contact with school staff, and an office adjacent to the parent/pupil entrance was considered important for this.

- Due to the need for excellent external connections, doors and thresholds to the outdoors needed to be easily controlled by staff, while maintaining safety for pupils and environmental comfort. Extensive external covered areas were located adjacent to access doors.

PRIMARY SCHOOL

....

A medium-sized primary school designed within a wider community building chose a class-based model arranged as a 'family group' to encourage cross-learning and the sharing of resources

As part of the development of a larger community building – providing a range of community facilities within a single 'block' of accommodation – a 75-pupil-entry primary school was proposed. The school decided to pursue a design model that grouped a series of spaces per year group to encourage communication and sharing.

Contextual facts

- School developed along a linear 'street'.

- Adjacent shared community facilities.

- 75-pupil-entry primary school for ages 5 to 11.

- Parkland setting.

Objectives

- Enable shared learning: the spaces should provide a forum for different groups to come together for shared activities, and to be able to break out into smaller groups for focused learning.

- Connect to related community uses: enable the pupils to use other community facilities as an extension of the activities of the school.

- Allow the sharing of teaching resources: the spaces should promote close collaboration between teachers to deliver the structured curriculum with access to shared resources.

Crucial choices

- Location: the school is based on a linear arrangement over two floors within a single block of multi-purpose accommodation such as sports facilities, public library, community rooms and so on. The building is within a parkland setting.

- Use: the facility is available for five to eleven year-olds, with 75 pupils per year group. Pre- and post-school activities are available within the wider community building.

- Layout: it was decided to gather each year group as a 'family' within a shared series of spaces acting as a 'neighbourhood'. Each year group exists as a defined unit within the school, with direct connections to shared spaces to encourage wider interaction with the school community.

PRIMARY SCHOOL

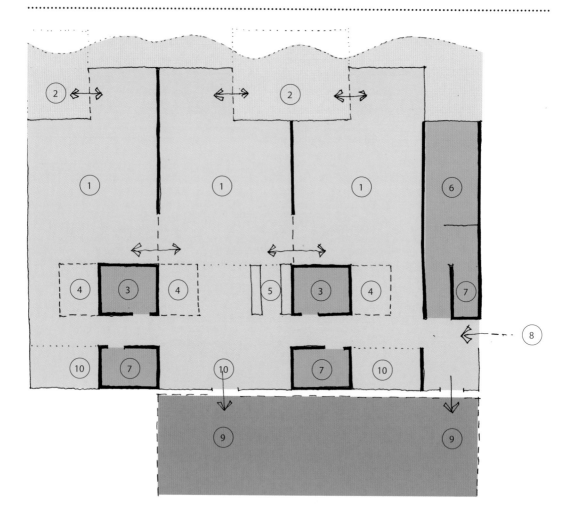

KEY
1. Class base
2. External covered area
3. Toilets
4. Cloakrooms
5. Wet zone
6. Staff
7. Resources
8. School connection
9. Connection to school 'heart' space
10. Group space

PRIMARY SCHOOL

- Appearance: the spaces are loosely open-plan, but zones are defined by fixed elements (for example, toilets) within the open-plan space. The space can be sub-divided into three zones for focused learning in smaller groups, but also can be opened up to form an articulated space with visual connections to encourage movement and interaction. Spaces around the fixed elements are intended to be easily reconfigurable by teachers and pupils. Floor and ceiling surfaces run continuously throughout to unify the space, with softer materials introduced in key areas to suggest gathering and use of the floor. The spaces are supported by acoustically absorptive materials in a variety of orientations to reduce reverberation and prevent disturbance between zones.

Learning spaces

The following types of learning space were considered to support the key objectives:

- Linked class-bases with the ability to be separated for focused group work.

- Direct communication to covered outdoor areas to encourage learning in all areas – internal and external.

- Central toilets and cloakroom areas that define learning zones.

- Dedicated staff office and resources area.

- Centralized wet facilities.

- Smaller group spaces, easily reconfigurable to support break out for focused learning and as thresholds to school 'heart' space.

Design solution

- The final design proposes a contained but open-plan year group space defined as a series of zones suitable for different group sizes.

- The year group spaces are clustered along a linear 'street' providing direct access to the school's 'heart' space, dining facilities and wider community uses (for example, sports facilities).

- Facilities are provided within the space for teachers to meet as a team and plan activities and assessments.

- A centralized wet area is provided adjacent to a meeting zone.

- The learning zones are designed to be further configured with loose furniture and flexible audio-visual solutions.

CONSIDERATIONS

- Direct connections to the school's large 'heart' space were important for staging shared school assemblies and for year groups to come together.

- Each year group can be sub-divided into three groups using sliding acoustic partitions when separate focused group work is required.

- Rather than provide wet areas throughout the space, wet facilities were centralized adjacent to an open area for group activities.

- A teacher resource and office was provided within the year group to enable collaboration and the planning of resources by the team of teachers working together.

- The entire neighbourhood is wifi-enabled with a number of display screens to encourage staff and pupils to share digital information from mobile devices.

SECONDARY SCHOOL

A 'transition' facility for pupils transferring from primary to secondary was proposed within a new school building to provide a model of learning that builds upon pupils' experiences of primary school and orientates them towards upper years

Pupils arriving at secondary school from primary school often struggle during their first year with the transition to new pedagogical practices. This new secondary school addressed this issue by proposing a transition facility for new pupils that acts in a fairly self-contained way and can support extended learning periods similar to primary learning spaces.

Contextual facts

- 'Transition' facility for 90 pupils aged 11–12 years within a new secondary school.
- School speciality in STEM subjects.
- Extended learning periods for transition pupils.

Objectives

- Provide an environment to support extended learning periods: the learning model requires longer periods for pupils within the space than an ordinary secondary school model. This requires a supportive environment where learning can be easily differentiated and provides spaces for focused group activities, reflecting the different needs of the pupils.
- Promote making and collaboration: access to a maker space/studio area should be allowed for pupils to explore ideas through making.
- Provide a variety of spaces for new pedagogical initiatives: the facility should provide a 'field of learning' with different spaces accommodating individual study, small-group activity and group presentation/gathering.

Crucial choices

- Location: the facility is located within a three-storey 'superblock' secondary school, with all accommodation in a single building block. The transition facility has been located on the ground floor adjacent to the school STEM spaces.
- Use: for 90 pupils aged 11–12 years, capable of being split into three separate classes or smaller groups. Whole-year gatherings occur in larger school rooms such as the assembly hall.

Opposite
Formal and informal spaces for a larger group of students. Mentone Grammar School, Keith Jones Learning Centre, Victoria, Australia

SECONDARY SCHOOL

- Layout: three zones for each class group are part of a loosely defined open-plan space, with fixed learning spaces such as group rooms providing opportunities for flexible audio-visual display. A stepped platform provides a space for gatherings and presentations.

- Appearance: ceiling, floor surfaces and lighting define learning zones within the larger space. Daylight and natural ventilation available throughout, with taller top-lit double-height space available over the stepped platform. Writeable walls are integrated with display zones, audio-visual equipment and acoustic panelling; these suggest areas where learners could gather, share ideas and connect with mobile technology. The acoustic environment is carefully controlled to reduce noise intrusion between different learning zones.

Learning spaces

The following types of learning space were considered to support the key objectives:

- Linked class-bases with the ability allow groups to share and collaborate.

- A stepped platform that can act as seating adjacent to an open space for presentation and can support more informal tasks.

- Group discussion spaces that can be enclosed for acoustic privacy.

- Small 'think' booths for individual or small-group study.

- A flexible maker space with art/design/technology resources.

Design solution

- The final design proposes a single facility of semi-open spaces that communicate across a shared area with shared resources.

- The facility has a defined 'entrance' and identity for transition-stage pupils.

- The learning zones are designed to be further configured with loose furniture and flexible audio-visual solutions.

- The environment is designed to support pupils for extended learning periods, and gives particular attention to levels of daylight, good levels of ventilation and lowered acoustic reverberation, as well as visual connections to the external landscape.

- Easy connections exist to wider school facilities and particularly to STEM spaces.

SECONDARY SCHOOL

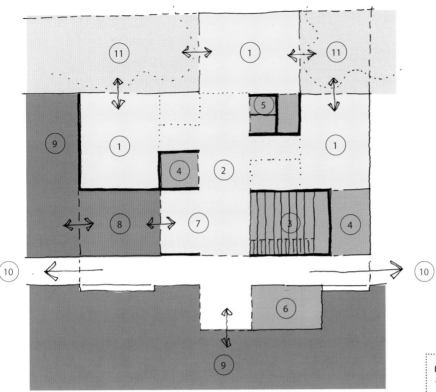

KEY

1. Class zone
2. Shared communication area
3. Stepped platform
4. Group discussion
5. Think booths
6. Staff
7. Presentation space
8. Maker space
9. STEM spaces
10. School connection
11. External terrace

CONSIDERATIONS

- The library, dining, toilets, lockers and other specialist spaces are located outside the transition facility to encourage interaction with other year groups.

- Maker space can open up to STEM spaces to act as a shared specialist area.

- Shared areas intended to be internal 'break-in' spaces for group work that can be supported by structured resources, wet area and so on.

- Staff office/resources located adjacent to the transition facility.

- Direct access to outdoor areas to extend learning opportunities and provide areas for pupils to enjoy.

- Access is available at the head of the stepped platform for upper-level entry to the transition space.

- IT based upon the use of mobile devices and charging points – no fixed IT suite required.

Overleaf
Albemarle County Public School, Virginia, USA

Equipping the Space

FURNITURE, FITTING-OUT
AND EQUIPMENT

ACOUSTICS AND INCLUSIVE
ENVIRONMENTS

FURNITURE, FITTING-OUT AND EQUIPMENT

....

Form, as they say, follows function. When that function was little more than to accommodate direct instruction, the form could be as simple as a table and chair – but as education evolves, things are getting more complex

Launched in 1963 following three years' research by designer Robin Day, the Hille Polyside chair remained the epitome of great school furniture design for around 30 years. Arranged in rows behind simple rectangular tables, seemingly the most important design features were that the chairs were lightweight, strong and could be stacked to enormous heights. And they were cheap, so much so that over 14 million have been made under licence in 30 countries around the world.

Today, furniture for learning spaces has necessarily become more sophisticated, taking in advances in ergonomics and neuroscience, as manufacturers have sought to support differing pedagogical approaches.

Zoning

As teachers started to identify different modes of learning and alter their practice accordingly, it became apparent that the single 'column and row' approach to furnishing learning spaces was no longer the panacea it might once have been considered. Lines of tables and chairs support didactic instruction reasonably well, but as teachers have integrated presentation, collaboration, research and contemplation into their lessons, it has become clear that one single, static furniture arrangement cannot adequately support all learning activities. And research, too, tells us that these different activities require different environments. It's therefore appropriate that different physical zones are created to support each, and that they're furnished so their functions are easily identifiable to learners.

Drawing on David Thornburg's *Campfires in Cyberspace*, we can conclude that learners need places to gather, collaborate, explore and reflect.

- Gather: focused spaces where everyone can see what they need to see, hear and be heard. Tiered seating here gives everyone uninterrupted lines of sight while also reducing the distance between the presenter and the back.

- Collaborate: agile spaces, enabling learners to rearrange furniture depending on what they're doing and who with. Dry-wipe surfaces, both vertical and horizontal, promote brainstorming and risk-taking.

- Explore: hands-on spaces where learners are encouraged to discover by doing. If they're too 'perfect', neuroscience tells us these spaces inhibit students from having a go, fearful of making a mistake or damaging something.

Opposite above
Making use of open spaces with a variety of furniture. Discovery Elementary School, Arlington, Virginia, USA

Opposite below
Divide the space with moveable walls. Carter G. Woodson Education Complex, Dillwyn, Virginia, USA

FURNITURE, FITTING-OUT AND EQUIPMENT

- Reflect: with some acoustic separation, these are spaces where learners can read, or just sit and think. They're spaces that understand and respect that we're unable to suppress auditory input and that this can impair attention.

Agility or adaptability

The changes in activity that lessons now incorporate mean that learners must be able to reconfigure furniture throughout the course of a lesson. This goes beyond merely putting wheels on everything – furniture needs to be modular and geometrically possible to arrange into different formats. For example, tables should be able to support group work of differing group sizes as well as whole-class discussion and direct instruction.

Agile, reconfigurable furniture must be much more robust than previously. For example, applied work-surface edges – ones that are bonded to the substrate – have fallen from favour. Instead, lacquered exposed ply, compact laminate and moulded polyurethane, while more expensive, are increasingly being used.

Multiple uses

It is important to recognize that not every space will be used at the same time. To counteract any perceived spatial inefficiency, furniture manufacturers have turned to 'sweating' the physical asset: enabling it to be used to its maximum and consequently making multi-use products especially relevant.

For example, height-adjustable, flip-top tables with dry-wipe surfaces can be used for groups to collaborate at, as well as (when tipped to vertical) for peer-to-peer presentation. Mobile cabinets can be used to demarcate spaces as well as provide storage close to hand. Seats, such as Steelcase's Node, can integrate storage, while benches of all heights (such as the Heppell Bench from Learniture® UK) can be used to sit at or sit on. Spaceoasis' Working Wall Lite brings dry-wipe surfaces and the ubiquitous Gratnells tray right into the classroom as a means of sub-dividing learning spaces while providing storage where it's needed. All these examples (and there are many more besides) are evidence that furniture items should be judged not by how robust or cheap they are but the extent to which they support learning and teaching.

Storage

This approach, of course, brings a new dimension to storage. Many teachers hoard resources, either because they want to keep things that have worked well to be able to reuse them in subsequent academic years or because they are fearful that limited financial budgets mean they will be unable to buy them again. A 'just-in-case' mentality frequently pervades teaching, while a collection of historically accumulated mismatched cupboards and filing cabinets are often used to store items in and on. However, research suggests that cluttered environments are a distraction, which prevent the learning spaces from operating at their optimum. Storage is one area where consistency is key, whether that is through the use of simple modular trays or a built-in 'teacher wall'. It is important that storage space is accessible to both students and teachers for project-based learning in more open areas. Project-based learning needs specific storage for ongoing work.

From top:
Series E chair designed by Robin Day for Hille

Bodyfurn® sled chair by Furnware

Hokki stool by VS

FURNITURE, FITTING-OUT AND EQUIPMENT

Building infrastructure

Furniture, fixtures and equipment (FF&E) should never be considered in isolation. It's inevitable, for example, that ICT devices will be placed on or at items of furniture, and will connect to the infrastructure of the building via an M&E (mechanical and electrical) strategy. For any of these approaches to be successful, they should be considered in parallel with the others. Mobile devices, for example, will have a different requirement to fixed ones both in terms of the furniture at which they're used and whether or not they require physical connectivity to power or data. All too often power and data is distributed via horizontal plastic trunking fixed approximately 900mm (35.5 inches) from the floor irrespective of what furniture or ICT it is used with. Wifi technology can make most of these problems obsolete.

Ergonomics and learning

Ergonomics is often misrepresented as relating solely to muscular-skeletal well-being; however, ergonomics can contribute significantly to cognition. Many of the assumptions that 'correct' sitting posture is when your joints are at broadly 90 degrees to each other can be traced back to the 1959 book *The Measure of Man* by Henry Dreyfuss, the American industrial designer. In it, Dreyfuss included numerous diagrams and associated measurements of people thus seated, and the book became widely accepted as the anthropometric 'bible' to which furniture manufacturers frequently referred for geometry and dimensions.

Today, with our improved understanding of how the human body works, we promote a seated posture where the thighs are dropped from the horizontal (in the 1980s the Alexander Technique kneeling chair was fashionable, although our knees are not the part of our body that have evolved to support our body weight). The easiest way to do this is to increase the height of the seat while detailing it to allow the thighs to drop. Simon Dennehy, of Dublin-based design consultancy Perch, used a deformable plastic seat to allow this to happen in his design for the Labofa Ray chair. Meanwhile, the Vitra Tip Ton chair allows the whole seat to tip forwards.

Ergonomically correct seating posture

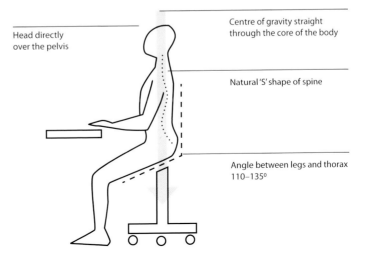

Head directly over the pelvis

Centre of gravity straight through the core of the body

Natural 'S' shape of spine

Angle between legs and thorax 110–135°

FURNITURE, FITTING-OUT AND EQUIPMENT

··

Dr Dieter Breithecker's 2005 report, *The Educational Workplace: What the 'classroom of the future' will look like*, included the results of a test he had conducted to measure concentration performance throughout the day in three classrooms. One was a 'traditional' controlled learning space; in another students had access to active play equipment during breaks; and in a third room the play equipment was in the learning space, enabling movement to be an intrinsic part of the lesson. Conducted over four years, students regularly underwent D2 cognitive skills tests at three specified times throughout the school day. In the control group, learners' cognition dropped throughout the day; in the second it was broadly level; and in the third the learners saw improvements in understanding the later it was in the day. Breithecker concluded that movement – and what he referred to as 'active sitting' – in fact aided cognition.

One reason for this finding might well be that most vital organs in the body are located in the lower thorax and that prolonged sitting with your thighs horizontal and abdomen vertical constricts the blood flow around these organs, which inhibits the flow of oxygen to the brain – contradicting the cliché 'sit still and concentrate'. In pretty well all other areas of life, activity is associated with health and well-being and is encouraged.

Because of the relatively rapid growth of primary-age students, it is more difficult to maintain sound ergonomic principles in younger children. It is not uncommon to see marked differences in stature between similarly aged children in the same class – yet they are typically required to be seated at the same size furniture. While there are standard sizes to which many manufacturers comply (such as DIN 1729 Part 1), the German manufacturer Vereinigte Spezialmöbelfabriken (VS) has recognized the fact that the distance between the seat and the work surface has remained, within some tolerance, fairly similar and has designed its Level seat to have an adjustable footrest. This allows smaller learners to sit comfortably at the same height table as taller learners.

Changes in concentration performance value (KL) in three different environments throughout the day

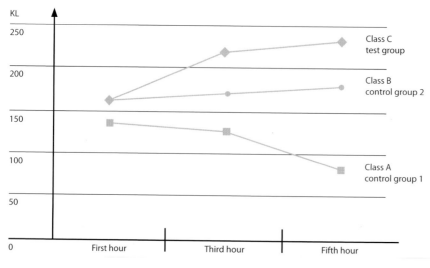

KL

250	Class C test group
200	Class B control group 2
150	
100	Class A control group 1
50	
0	First hour · Third hour · Fifth hour

FURNITURE, FITTING-OUT AND EQUIPMENT

According to neuroscientist Dr Tim Holmes of London's Royal Holloway University, tiered seating is another furniture solution that aids concentration: 'It's all too easy to think attention is something students have complete control over, but in fact maintaining attention requires significant resources in the brain. Innovations like tiered seating improve social attention for both the student and the teacher by providing clear lines of sight, making it easier for the student to focus on the information being delivered with an inevitable improvement on learning outcomes.' On top of this, by virtue of the students sitting on different levels, those at the back are, in fact, closer to the orator than in a traditional classroom. Numerous versions of tiered seating exist, from EromesMarko's simple glass-fibre 'Amfi' through to retractable upholstered units such as Martela's 'BEATBOX' designed by Liro Viljanen.

Dry-wipe surfaces

As ICT becomes a utility rather than a novelty, the visceral, instinctive action of picking up a pen and making a physical mark on a surface has regained its relevance. Schools have moved towards the use of both horizontal and vertical dry-wipe surfaces, no longer constrained by conventional whiteboard sizes. Smartphones can then be used to upload photos of the work to digital portfolios.

There are numerous ways, each with advantages and disadvantages, in which vertical surfaces can be made dry-wipe: paint, for example, while relatively inexpensive and seamless, relies on the quality of the wall to which it is applied. However, maintenance can be expensive. Many schools construct storage and resource areas with a high-gloss dry-wipe surface as part of the design. The quality and durability of dry-wipe surfaces is developing fast, and there are now flexible sheets that can be applied to surfaces.

Below
The wall as a whiteboard.
Eton College, Windsor, UK

ACOUSTICS AND INCLUSIVE ENVIRONMENTS

Getting the sound right in a learning space can pay off for everyone, especially children with autism and other special needs

An optimal sound environment is a basic necessity if all students are to learn effectively. The modern classroom puts greater emphasis on group communication and collaboration, which often increases the overall noise level. When the sound environment is optimal it will improve comfort, focus and the quality of both learning and teaching.

There is, then, a real incentive to improve acoustics in teaching spaces: optimal acoustics means better communication and reduced stress for both staff and students, leading to better academic results. It is also worth bearing in mind that government standards tend to be minimum standards. The acoustics of the learning environment should be based on how people experience sound and the way it affects them, not just on meeting minimum formal standards.

Also, as a quality that is desired, acoustics is usually second only to natural light. In 2015, Hawkins Brown Architects, in collaboration with other industry professionals, launched *Great Schools*, which was very well received by the education sector. The book claimed: 'A well-proportioned classroom which has appropriate storage, with just the right amount of display, is flooded with natural light, has good acoustics, no glare, good air quality, a comfortable temperature, and sufficient space to accommodate a range of activities for the right number of students, will improve educational outcomes.'

A growing challenge in the design of schools is autism, which is much more common than many people think. Some students with autism are highly sensitive to loud noise, echo (reverberation) or multiple sound signals, with the inability to filter out sounds. Acoustic separation and a calming, peaceful learning space can help staff to maintain an inclusive environment.

CONSIDERATIONS

- Keep the room size down. Reverberation naturally increases with room volume, so large rooms need more acoustic treatment. Children with special educational needs (SEN) should generally be taught in smaller classes.

- For the same reason, keep the ceiling height lower. Things become more difficult above 2.8 metres (9 feet 2 inches) in height because reflections from the walls become problematic, not having been absorbed by the ceiling.

- Use only absorptive finishes that meet 'Type A' (the highest classification for absorption) because these are the most efficient and reduce the area of absorption required.

- If possible, use dry-lined walls because these also provide some useful bass absorption at no additional cost. The effects of absorbing or diffusing furniture and fittings can also be helpful.

- A conventional suspended ceiling tile is most efficient and provides some bass absorption, but designing for SEN may require the use of proprietary 'bass absorbing pads'.

Opposite above
Storage walls and glazing to create quiet learning zones. Witzenhausen School, Germany

Opposite below
Diagrammatic representation of a traditional classroom with appropriate acoustic treatment

Optimum height: 2.8m (9ft 2in)

ACOUSTICS AND INCLUSIVE ENVIRONMENTS

Recently, a number of European schools have focused on the benefits of good acoustic design. At the world-renowned De Werkplaats school in Bilthoven, The Netherlands, the new extension was designed in line with the philosophy of Kees Boeke by abandoning the traditional idea of classrooms. The result was a brand-new school building in which the classes are taught in one connected but zoned 'open learning environment'.

Moving the desks around has become a thing of the past in this school: 'Each corner of the school is designed for a certain activity. So if we're doing arts and crafts, we go to the studio. Children who are easily distracted go to the quiet area of the building. Having the children move around this way saves having to adapt the classroom.' This design approach reflects the pedagogy and the organization of the curriculum experience through a collaborative approach to learning.

A lot of noise might be expected in an area housing 300 schoolchildren, but nothing could be further from the truth at De Werkplaats. That the school is not noisy is due to the forethought of architect Kees Willems, who focused on the acoustics element of the building design.

Of course, children are an important part of the acoustic equation too. Where they have appropriate protocols and behaviours, noise is less. Arming the children with the data that reflects their noise – a simple decibel meter app on an old tablet perhaps – and asking two students to be Sound Monitors for the day helps them to own, and minimize, their acoustic environments. Similarly, zoning a learning space so that there is a section for quiet work, a place for pairs to collaborate or using a corner with tiered seating for whole-class instruction will all reduce noise considerably and improve the learning too. Children love the science of learning. Remember to let them be an active part of the solution.

Opposite above
Creating acoustic alcoves. Werkplaats Kindergemeenschap, Bilthoven, Netherlands

Opposite below
Acoustic zones in open-plan areas. Werkplaats Kindergemeenschap, Bilthoven, Netherlands

Overleaf
Hazel Wolf K-8, Seattle, Washington, USA

The ideal heat, light and sound levels for learning

- Temperature: 18–21 degrees Celsius (64–70 degrees Fahrenheit).

- Lighting: Above 250 lux for engaged conversation; above 450 lux for close work such as writing.

- Sound: Above 72 decibels starts to be disruptive.

- CO_2: High levels (from 1,000 parts per million) of CO_2 will affect concentration.

All figures thanks to Professor Stephen Heppell. More at www.learnometer.net.

CONSIDERATIONS

- If there can't be a suspended ceiling, consider suspended baffles or 'rafts'. These are very efficient because both sides are absorptive, but they are not great at low frequencies, so you will need more bass absorption from wall panels.

- It is more challenging but not impossible to achieve an optimal SEN acoustic environment in spaces where the soffit is left exposed as part of the thermal strategy.

- Whatever the ceiling type, acoustically absorptive wall panels will be needed as well.

At least some of these should be at ear height, so they will need to be robust.

- Conventional 'Sabine' calculations are unreliable for larger, connected, open or semi-open spaces. To ensure the design is right, a 3-D acoustic computer model will be needed.

- Acoustics consultants who are experienced in this type of design should be involved early in the project to advise on room shapes and sizes. They should also be involved in the final delivery of the space and the post-occupancy evaluation of its use.

mohorovicic
discontinuity

lo
(partia

weake

The Importance of Research

POST-OCCUPANCY EVALUATION

LEARNING FROM THE
WORK OF OTHERS

INTELLIGENT CLASSROOM
DESIGN CAN IMPROVE
LEARNING OUTCOMES

IMPLEMENTING YOUR VISION

POST-OCCUPANCY EVALUATION

Open-plan teaching spaces are more than just large classrooms, they need to reflect the approach to learning and teaching in the school. But how effective are these spaces in practice?

From post-occupancy evaluation (POE) studies, it is clear that the schools and design teams that embrace the concepts of open-plan teaching are those that achieve the benefits. For example, within a series of schools in Kent, UK, open-plan spaces were encouraged at a high level, but during the course of procurement – because of staff changes and gradual misinterpretation of the principles – the open-plan spaces became simply classrooms without walls. Instead of large groups being taught as one, up to three separate classes were being taught independently within the same space. With judicious teacher scheduling and training these spaces were made to work, but they were rarely used with the more dynamic teaching styles they were originally intended for.

In schools where the open-plan format has been successful, a mix of spaces is provided, each connected to the central, large teaching space. This creates the variety that is needed to be able to benefit from flexible teaching methods.

These ancillary spaces are most successful when they are enclosed, creating a barrier to noise between spaces and allowing complete autonomy. This has proved very useful when teacher-led, or for loud group work, but the lack of open lines of sight into these closed spaces restricts their use for unsupervised learning.

At Plymouth School of Creative Arts in the UK, breakout spaces within the building's circulation routes become the supplementary teaching spaces. Their high visibility ensures that they can be safely used for self-guided learning or group work. Using the circulation routes for learning is an efficient way to justify generous, large avenues through the building.

Acoustics is the key design aspect to get right with more-open and connected learning spaces. Extensive acoustic absorption is often required, along with careful zoning of the building into quiet/loud areas.

Including open-plan spaces can lead to a very efficient school area, with fewer internal walls that would otherwise reduce the usable area. This additional space can be very appealing, particularly in terms of cost, but it is worth planning how the space could be enclosed to form more typical classrooms or studio spaces.

When designing open spaces that could be closed in at a future date, each potential enclosure will need access to a window for daylight. It is particularly useful to design out beams and include flat floors and soffits that can accommodate walls in any location in order to increase future adaptability.

POST-OCCUPANCY EVALUATION

The building that is most successful is the one that effortlessly enables the desired approach to learning and teaching. While the physical structure can act as a catalyst for pedagogical change, success has to be driven by the approach of everyone at every level.

In developing a brief for a new space, it is necessary to understand how existing environments perform, and the best place to start is by looking at post-occupancy evaluations (POEs). A POE provides key feedback at the end of a project, forging that feedback loop between the design and the operation of a space. POEs are commonly used following handover, as the building settles in and the occupants find their particular way of working in their new space. The POE process establishes how the building can be shaped to further improve outcomes.

POEs, by necessity, have a very broad remit and can be fitted to meet the needs of the occupants and the designers. The two common themes of a POE are finding out how satisfied the occupant is and the energy performance of the building. Interviews and questionnaires can provide rich, detailed subjective findings, but a true picture of occupant satisfaction requires objective environmental monitoring. How happy an occupant really is with their space can be determined by measuring everything from simple temperature to reverberation times and monitoring of specific air pollutants. Once the occupant's patterns are understood, the energy performance can be examined, aiming to reduce the energy consumption while improving the occupant's satisfaction.

The process of post-occupancy review

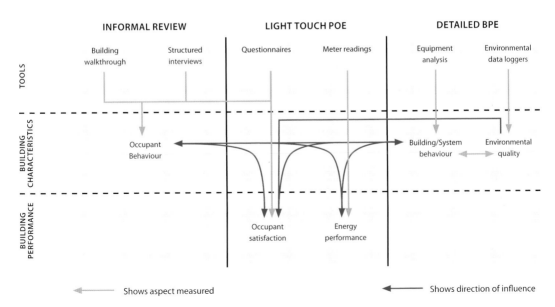

LEARNING FROM THE WORK OF OTHERS

Research into the effects of learning spaces is now recognized internationally. Important work is being carried out in schools by major academic institutions across the globe

One of the largest current series of projects is the University of Melbourne's Learning Environments Applied Research Network (LEaRN), which brings together academia and industry. Within this network, the Innovative Learning Environments and Teacher Change project (ILETC) is looking at space through the lens of learning and teaching. It examines performance in actual built learning spaces rather than theorizing from afar. The aim here is to provide practical guidance for teachers in particular, but inevitably there is advice for designers, and much of it is on the design and planning of learning space.

The Organisation for Economic Co-operation and Development (OECD) has been engaged with policy and research into learning environments since 1972. Its School User Survey, published in 2018, was developed under its Learning Environments Evaluation Programme (LEEP) to generate insights into how students and teachers use learning spaces in practice. Using self-assessment questionnaires for students, teachers and school leaders, the aim is to support continuous improvement at school level. The survey is open for use by any school or group of schools. Not only will this feed into general data about how school buildings are being used, but it will also enable schools to see how they perform. Alongside case studies of school improvement that are being developed, teachers, school leaders and designers will be able to look at how they can make changes in their existing school.

A third area of research is through some of the development banks. The World Bank and the Inter-American Development Bank (IADB), in particular, are publishing some of their background work. Indeed, the World Bank is publishing a new review of the literature on the impact of buildings on student outcome. Meanwhile, the IADB has gathered over 80 examples of new school buildings.

A crucial source of research is that undertaken by practitioners, either as specific projects or as part of their work, and more of this needs to be published. The evaluation of a school building project after completion, to see how it supports the needs of its users now and in the future, needs to be better established. Very often, under the heading 'post-occupancy evaluation', this evaluation considers merely the technical features of the building and not how the user interacts with the space. A fully integrated approach should be essential as a natural part of the project cycle.

There are now extensive studies on the value of movement within a learning space and its impact on outcomes.

Opposite
Circular school taking advantage of articulated classrooms. University of Cambridge Primary School, Cambridge, UK

INTELLIGENT CLASSROOM DESIGN CAN IMPROVE LEARNING OUTCOMES

Sceptics were proved wrong when researchers successfully showed that classroom design makes a difference to student results

It was a complex task for Professor Peter Barrett to establish the link between the design of a classroom and rates of learning. In fact, his team of researchers at the University of Salford took eight years.

A survey, which included 3,766 children in 137 classrooms from 27 very different schools, eventually provided firm evidence that the physical characteristics of the classroom accounted for 16 per cent of the variation in the learning progress of these children. Details of the large study are given in a peer-reviewed journal, *Building and Environment*, and in an illustrated guide for designers and teachers, entitled 'Clever Classrooms'.

To separate the impact of the space itself from other factors, Barrett's HEAD (Holistic Evidence and Design) study did two things. First, it focused on primary schools, where the pupils are mainly in the same classroom for the whole year. This meant that any possible impact would be maximized and also that there would be strong metrics of their academic progress. Second, multi-level statistical modelling was used to differentiate the impacts of the classroom itself from variations owing to individual pupil differences or whole-school effects.

In addition, the HEAD study takes an approach that places the pupil at the centre of the analysis. This includes everything (as far as possible) that impacts on the pupil through their senses and is interpreted by their brain. This led to the development of the 'SIN' (stimulation–individualization–naturalness) framework of factors to be considered.

- Stimulation: visual complexity and colour.

- Individualization: ownership (personalization and distinctiveness), the flexibility of the layout and connection (or way-finding).

- Naturalness: light, temperature, air quality, sound and links to nature.

It can be seen that the naturalness factors are fairly familiar, and it turns out that these are very important, collectively accounting for about half of the impact of the classroom on learning. More novel and surprising is the clear finding that the individualization and stimulation factors, taken together, are equally important. They each drive about a quarter of the impact on learning.

To learn optimally, pupils need classroom spaces that are healthy (naturalness), distinctive, allow ownership and personalization (individualization), and that present an appropriate level of ambient stimulation. This last factor is the result of a combination of the visual complexity of the space and of the colour scheme. The HEAD study clearly showed for the first time that in practice a mid-level of stimulation is ideal for learning, not too boring or too chaotic.

Below
A summary of the impacts associated with the seven design parameters found to be statistically important

Stimulation
Complexity
Colour

Individualization
Ownership
Flexibility

Naturalness
Light
Temperature
Air Quality

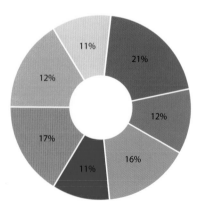

11%
21%
12%
12%
16%
11%
17%

INTELLIGENT CLASSROOM DESIGN CAN IMPROVE LEARNING OUTCOMES

Considerable effort was taken to include school-level factors, such as the layout of the school and outside play facilities, but the variation between classrooms within each school tended to be greater than the aggregate differences between schools. In short, in terms of learning progress, the primary school pupil's classroom is their world – and as such that is where effort needs to be focused when investing in the infrastructure. This does not mean that other broader factors should be ignored, but it argues strongly for making sure that each (existing or proposed) classroom works in its own right and from there to build out to a broader picture. This could be styled 'inside-out' design and is captured by the idea that there are rarely good or bad schools, rather there are more- and less-effective classrooms. That is the detailed level of analysis needed to bring about improvements that will impact on the educational progress of pupils.

The naturalness design parameters of good (day)lighting, and control over temperature and ventilation are all important in relation to learning. So windows should not be covered with display material, individual classrooms should have local thermostats and windows should be opened when rooms are getting stuffy.

The more novel individualization design parameters of flexibility and ownership are, respectively, about offering options to pupils and teachers to create a personal connection with their classroom. Some of this is about the spaces created within and adjacent to the classroom. These can support a variety of activities, which is especially important for younger children where the teaching methods are typically more play-based.

Below
Professor Barrett considers the stimulation effects of the wall display

Even in a rectangular room, learning zones (for example, for reading, art, role play) can be established with the creative use of furniture. Without this infrastructure it is hard for teachers to deliver the curriculum in an interesting and engaging way. Ownership can come from visible signs of the pupils – their work on display boards on the wall, their names on trays, and so on. Additionally, the classroom furniture should be age-appropriate and of good quality. At one level this seems to send a message to the children that they are valued, while at a practical level a child is not going to be comfortable if sitting on a chair and at a desk that are too big for them. In Norway, for example, it is absolutely normal for all pupils to have height-adjustable chairs. The aim is to get to the point where the pupils are comfortable ergonomically and clearly feel that 'this is our classroom'.

The other novel area concerns the appropriate level of stimulation. Visual complexity can come from the shape and form of the room, which can be addressed through the basic structure or via learning zones. Stimulation can also be strongly driven by the extent and coherence of displays. Walls, floors, furniture and blinds all contribute, but for walls, typically a light, calm general colour plus an area of brighter colour, maybe on the 'teaching wall', can work well.

Overall, the HEAD findings mean that it is now a practical proposition for architects, teachers and designers to look at each classroom as an active contributor to the learning process.

IMPLEMENTING YOUR VISION

Who wants to be the architect that builds the last 'old school' school?

Innovation in school design is not a 'nice to have', it's a necessity. To re-create the factory model buildings of the past will not only fail future generations, it will embed failure. The future requires a rethink on curricula and the spaces in which they are taught. It's not about optimizing schooling, it's about optimizing learning.

A school is not a static space, it is a structure that should be sensitive to and responsive to both the internal and external environments, with the ability to adapt and evolve. Space and pedagogy go hand in hand.

The learning spaces you are about to design need to be resilient and versatile enough to empower all types of learners. The roles of teachers and students are evolving and relationships will change. Carefully consider a move from teacher-directed classroom practice to a teacher-enabled approach. Create spaces that allow teachers to interact with students, peers and the community.

Students are engaged and enabled through a more personalized curriculum experience, and therefore the space in which they learn should be flexible, imaginative and dynamic.

The design should be driven and shaped throughout the process by constantly posing the questions, why? and how?

Develop the planning of learning spaces through a consultative, collaborative and research-based approach. After all, who wants to be the architect that builds the last 'old school' school?

Opposite
Learning is fun

REFERENCE

Further reading

Barrett, Professor Peter; Zhang, Dr Yufan; Davies, Dr Fay; and Barrett, Dr Lucinda. 'Clever Classrooms', summary of the HEAD (Holistic Evidence and Design) Project, University of Salford, 2015

Barrett, Professor Peter; Zhang, Dr Yufan; Moffat, Joanne; and Kobbacy, Khairy. 'A holistic, multi-level analysis identifying the impact of classroom design on pupils' learning', published in *Building and Environment* journal, Volume 59, January 2013

Bechtel, Robert B. *Enclosing Behavior.* (Vol. 31.) John Wiley & Sons, 1977

Breithecker, Dr Dieter. 'The Educational Workplace: What the "classroom of the future" will look like', Bundesarbeitsgemeinschaft für Haltungs und Bewegungsförderung e. V, 2005. Paper available for download at http://www.benchmarque.ca/uploads/1/9/1/0/19103409/future_classroom_article.pdf

Doorley, Scott and Witthoft, Scott. *Make Space: How to Set the Stage for Creative Collaboration*, John Wiley & Sons, 2012

Dreyfuss, Henry. *The Measure of Man: Human Factors in Design*, Whitney Library of Design, 1960

Dunbar, Roger L.M. and Starbuck, William H. 'Learning to Design Organizations and Learning from Designing Them' in *Organization Science*, Volume 17, Issue 2, March–April 2006. See article at https://pubsonline.informs.org/doi/abs/10.1287/orsc.1060.0181

Gronn, Peter and Biddulph, James. (Editors.) *A University's Challenge: Cambridge's Primary School for the Nation*, Cambridge University Press, 2016

Hawkins Brown Architects in partnership with *The Architects' Journal. Great Schools: Making the Case for Good Design*, 2015. Available for download at https://www.hawkinsbrown.com/cms/documents/GreatSchools_forweb.pdf

Horn, Michael B. and Staker, Heather. *Blended: Using Disruptive Innovation to Improve Schools*, Jossey-Bass, 2014

Mirchandani, Nick and Wright, Sharon. (Editors.) *Future Schools: Innovative Design for Existing and New Buildings*, RIBA Publishing, 2015

Mitra, Sugata. 'Sole Toolkit: How to bring self-organised learning environments to your community', School in the Cloud, 2015. Available for download at www.schoolinthecloud.org, link: https://s3-eu-west-1.amazonaws.com/school-in-the-cloud-production-assets/toolkit/SOLE_Toolkit_Web_2.6.pdf

Organisation for Economic Co-operation and Development (OECD). 'Improving Learning Spaces Together: OECD School User Survey 2018'. Available for download at http://www.oecd.org/education/OECD-School-User-Survey-2018.pdf

Organisation for Economic Co-operation and Development (OECD). 'What makes a school a learning organisation?: A guide for policy makers, school leaders and teachers'. Available for download at http://www.oecd.org/education/school/school-learning-organisation.pdf

Papert, Seymour. *Mindstorms: Children, Computers, and Powerful Ideas*, Basic Books, 1993.

Papert, Seymour. *The Children's Machine: Rethinking School in the Age of the Computer*, Basic Books, 1994

Schein, Edgar H. *Organizational Culture and Leadership*, Jossey-Bass, 2004. Available for download at http://www.untag-smd.ac.id/files/Perpustakaan_Digital_2/ORGANIZATIONAL%20CULTURE%20Organizational%20Culture%20and%20Leadership,%203rd%20Edition.pdf

Seldon, Anthony with Oladimeji Abidoye. *The Fourth Education Revolution: Will Artificial Intelligence Liberate or Infantilise Humanity?*, The University of Buckingham Press, 2018

Strudwick, D. *Educating Children with Emotional and Behavioural Difficulties*, Routledge Falmer, 2002

Thornburg, David D. *Campfires in Cyberspace: Primordial Metaphors for Learning in the 21st Century*, Starsong Publications, 1999. Related handout download available from the Thornburg Center for Professional Development: http://tcpd.org/Thornburg/Handouts/Campfires.pdf

Wenger, Étienne. *Communities of Practice: Learning, Meaning, and Identity*, Cambridge University Press, 1998

REFERENCE

Other sources

The Association for Science Education
www.ase.org.uk
https://www.ase.org.uk/resources/
lab-design

Ben Barber Innovation Academy
https://bbcta.mansfieldisd.org/

**Caulfield Grammar School
Learning Project**
https://www.caulfieldgs.vic.edu.au/
https://www.hayball.com.au/projects/
caulfield-grammar-school-learning-
project/

The Clayton Christensen Institute
https://www.christenseninstitute.org/
about/

DEGW Archive at the University of
Reading (DEGW, the design agency
founded by Dr Francis Duffy in 1973, is
now part of Aecom)

**Hille, the Polyside chair
designed by Robin Day**
https://www.hille.co.uk/polyside-chair

Iletc
www.iletc.com.au

Learning by Design, Australia
*New Learning: Transformational Designs
for Pedagogy and Assessment*
http://newlearningonline.com/learning-
by-design/about-learning-by-design

OECD School User Survey
www.oecd.org/education/innovation-
education/centreforeffectivelearning
environmentscele/

Plymouth School of Creative Arts
https://plymouthschoolofcreativearts.co.uk/

Rosan Bosch Studio, Copenhagen
http://www.rosanbosch.com/en

School in the Cloud
www.schoolinthecloud.org

South Melbourne Primary School
https://www.schoolbuildings.vic.gov.au/
schools/Pages/SouthMelbournePrimary
School.aspx

University of Melbourne
Innovative Learning Environments
and Teacher Change (ILETC)
https://research.unimelb.edu.au/
learnetwork/projects/iletc

Learning Environments Applied
Research Network (LEaRN),
https://research.unimelb.edu.au/
learnetwork

Programme on International Student
Assessment (PISA)

Wenger, Étienne
http://wenger-trayner.com/introduction-
to-communities-of-practice/

De Werkplaats School
http://www.wpkeesboeke.nl/

West Thornton Primary Academy
http://thesynaptictrust.org/our-schools/
west-thornton-primary-academy

INDEX

••

Note: page numbers in *italics*
refer to illustrations.

A

acoustic considerations 122–5, 128
adaptable design 34, 118
AI (artificial intelligence) 83
Albemarle County Public School, Virginia,
  USA *114*, *115*
applied and technical learning 87–91
art studios 75
articulated classrooms *46*, 47–8
artificial intelligence (AI) 83
Australia *31*, *50*, *53*, *54*, 56–7, *110*, 130

B

Barfield, Julia 48
Barrett, Peter 132, *133*
Bechtel, Robert 51
Bedales School Orchard Development,
  Hampshire, UK *18*
Ben Barber Innovation Academy in
  Mansfield, Texas, USA 88
Billund, Denmark *59*
Blavatnik Building, Tate Modern 75
Breithecker, Dieter 120
Brighton Secondary College, Victoria,
  Australia *54*
BYOP (Bring Your Own Plant to school) *31*

C

career and technical education (CTE)
  88–91
Carter G. Woodson Education Complex,
  Dillwyn, Virginia, USA *117*
Carter G. Woodson School, Virginia, USA
  66
Caulfield Grammar School, Australia 56–7
central spaces 93, *100*
circulation spaces 101, 128
classrooms
  see learning spaces
Clayton Christensen Institute 83
collaborative design 19–20, 27, 63
collaborative spaces 33–4, *54*, 57, *82*, 93,
  96, 116
communities of practice 55
community involvement 63, 107
computers
  see information and
    communications technology (ICT)
concentration performance value (KL) 120
connectivity (spatial) 48, *49*, 52, 101
creative arts 75
CTE (career and technical education)
  88–91

D

Dame Bradbury's School, Saffron Walden,
  UK *103*
dance studios 76
Day, Robin 116

daylighting 122
Denmark *22*, 24, 39, 40, *43*, *59*
Dennehy, Simon 119
design constraints 20
design objectives 15
design parameters 132
design process 21
digital resources 58, 61
digital technologies 78–81
disability
  see inclusivity
Discovery Elementary School, Arlington,
  VA, USA *36*, *62*, *117*
drama studios 76
Dreyfuss, Henry 119
dry-wipe surfaces 121
Dulwich College, London, UK *71*
Dunbar, Robin 55

E

early years 45–50, 104–6
environmental considerations 125,
  132, 133
ergonomics and learning 119–20
Eton College, Windsor, UK *121*
external spaces
  see outdoor learning

F

family engagement 63
fire safety 68
flexibility 34, 51, 52, 118
Forest Schools 48, 104
Freemans Bay School, Auckland, New
  Zealand *12*, *94*, 95
furniture 34, 116–21, *117*, 133
  for digital technologies 81
  ergonomics and learning 119–20
  laboratory 70
  media space 85

G

The Gardens School, Auckland, New
  Zealand *60*
gathering spaces *53*, 93, *96*, 116
Gene A. Buinger Career and Technical
  Education Academy, Bedford, Texas,
  USA *86*, *91*
Georgetown High School, Texas, USA *89*
Germany *123*
Greensward Academy, Hockley, UK *64*

H

Hawkins Brown Architects 122
Hazel Wolf K-8, Seattle, Washington, USA
  92, *96*, *126*
HEAD (Holistic Evidence and Design) 7,
  132–3
'heart' space 93
Hertzberger, Herman 9, 47
High-Tech High, San Diego, California,
  USA *89*

Holistic Evidence and Design (HEAD) 7,
  132–3
Holmes, Tim 121
Horn, Michael B. 83
Høsterkøb School, Høsterkøb, Denmark
  22, *43*
hubs 56, *56*, 93
Hudson, Murray 7

I

ICT (information and communications
  technology) 78–81, 119
inclusivity 122
individualization 13–14, 83, 132
indoor environment 125, 132, 133
information and communications
  technology (ICT) 78–81, 119
Innovative Learning Environments and
  Teacher Change project (ILETC) 130
inside/outside learning 20, 42, 45, *49*, 106
  see also outdoor learning
Inter-American Development Bank (IADB)
  130
Italy 47

L

laboratories 68–71, 88
Lairdsland Primary School, Kirkintilloch,
  Scotland, UK *49*
layouts
  see spatial layouts
learning communities 52, 55
learning cultures 22–3, 25, 39
Learning Environments Applied Research
  Network (LEaRN) 130
learning hubs 56, *56*, 93
learning landscapes *38*, *41*, 52
learning methods 33–4, 39–40
learning neighbourhoods 55
learning outcomes 132–3
learning resources 58, 61
learning spaces 23–4, 29
  articulated classrooms *46*, 47–8
  connecting 48, *49*, 52, 101, 107–9
  defining 51–2
  diversity 40
  flexible 34, 51, 51–2, 118
  spatial requirements 51
  specialist 67–91
  types 106, 109, 112
    see also learning zones;
    spatial layouts
learning zones 24, 33–5, 57, 109,
  116–18, 133
library spaces 58–61, *59*, *60*, *62*, *103*
Liceo Europa, Zaragoza, Spain *38*, *41*
lighting 122

M

maker spaces 72, 87–8
Malaguzzi, Loris 7, 47
Marks Barfield Architects 48
media space 85

CONTRIBUTORS

Professor Peter Barrett is an emeritus professor of property and construction management. His work on the impact of the value of the built environment within society led him to study the connection between the physical design of schools and pupils' academic progress. This focus led him to becoming an Honorary Research Fellow in the Department of Education at Oxford University. As well as holding many strategy/policy roles nationally and internationally, he is past President of the UN-established International Council for Research and Innovation in Building and Construction. He now works as an independent researcher in the school design arena, for clients in the UK and abroad.
www.peterbarrettresearch.co.uk

Alastair Blyth
(Learning from the work of others)
is a senior lecturer and architect with a specific research interest in learning environments. His personal blog site is Re-Imagine Space for Learning. He is a Course Leader for Professional Practice Architecture, the RIBA Part 3 post-graduate programme.
alastair-blyth.com

Rosan Bosch
(Designing for pre-school and early years)
is a Dutch-born artist who has worked professionally with art, design and architecture for more than 20 years. Her interdisciplinary agency, Rosan Bosch Studio, was founded in Copenhagen in 2011 and it works in the crossover between art, architecture and design. Among its designs are the renowned Vittra Telefonplan School and Vittra Brotorp School in Sweden, Liceo Europa in Spain and Sheikh Zayed Private Academy in Abu Dhabi.
http://www.rosanbosch.dk

Professor Andrew Brewerton *(Art)*
is Principal & Chief Executive and Professor of Plymouth College of Art, founding Chair of Governors of Plymouth School of Creative Arts, Distinguished Professor of Shanghai Academy of Fine Art and Visiting Professor of the School of Fine Arts at Nanjing Normal University. Andrew has served on numerous national bodies; for example as Vice-Chair of Guild HE, as a member of the National Council of Arts Council England and the Creative Industry Federation's UK Advisory Council, and as Vice-Chair of the Prime Minister's Initiative in Higher Education. He is an English graduate of the University of Cambridge and a poet and writer on contemporary art.

Chadwickdryerclarke Studio
(How the spaces can come together)
is a RIBA Chartered Practice of architects based in Cambridge, UK. Founded in 2013 by Robin Dryer, Mark Clarke and Delphine Dryer, the practice has developed a specialism in designing for education, and through its work with educationalists retains a wide interest in the relationship of pedagogy and space. Key projects include the Rising Path for the Cambridge University Botanic Garden, the New Sports and Learning Building for the Stephen Perse Foundation and Cherry Hinton Hall for Cambridge International School.
http://www.chadwickdryerclarke.co.uk/

James Clarke
(Furniture, fitting-out and equipment)
is a specialist in furniture, fixtures and equipment (FF&E), who graduated from Ravensbourne with a degree in Furniture Design in 1986. Since 2004 he has specified furniture for learning environments in schools, colleges and universities, both as an independent FF&E consultant as well as on behalf of leading furniture manufacturers, working on major capital projects via construction consortia as well as directly with education institutions. He edits *Learning Spaces* magazine on behalf of *Teaching Times*.
www.learniture.co.uk

Peter Clegg of Feilden Clegg Bradley (FCB) Studios is regarded as a pioneer in environmental design, with over 40 years' experience in low-energy architecture. His involvement in schools projects includes an Academy in Bangladesh as well as a series of award-winning schools: Chelsea Academy, St Mary Magdalene Academy and Plymouth School of Creative Arts. His work in the education sector led him to become primary author of *Learning from Schools*, which focuses on FCB Studios' award-winning school-building programme. He was made Royal Designer for Industry (RDI) in 2010.
http://fcbstudios.com

Michál Cohen
(How to approach school design)
is a director and co-founder of Walters & Cohen Architects, a London-based practice that has completed many highly acclaimed education buildings. Michál believes that learning environments should be stimulating, fun and flexible, allowing teachers and pupils to teach and learn in the ways that suit them best. She is inspired by education design around the world and developments in pedagogical thinking, both of which influence her innovative and well-loved designs.
http://waltersandcohen.com

Shane Cryer
(Acoustics and inclusive environments)
manages the education sector in the UK and Ireland for the Swedish acoustic experts, Ecophon. After a career in the construction industry, having studied building and property surveying, he now concentrates on building acoustics. Working closely with organizations such as the Institute of Acoustics (IOA) and the Royal Institute of British Architects (RIBA), Shane has been promoting the new Building Bulletin 93 (BB93): Acoustic Design of Schools standard via CPD seminars, conferences and articles in the trade press. Shane also manages several acoustic research projects around the UK.
www.ecophon.com

Herman Hertzberger
(Foreword)
is one of the most important Dutch architects and theoreticians of the modern age. Hertzberger built many school buildings during his long career, including the Montessori School in Delft (1966, expanded repeatedly), the Apollo (1983) and De Evenaar (1986) schools in Amsterdam, Polygoon in Almere (1992) and the Anne Frank school in Papendrecht (1994). Hertzberger has written several books, including *Lessons for Students in Architecture* (1991), *Space and the Architect: Lessons in Architecture 2* (1999) and *Space and Learning* (2008).
www.hertzberger.nl

CONTRIBUTORS

Lene Jensby Lange
(How to begin)
is a passionate educational entrepreneur who brings people and minds together to reimagine the future of learning. She founded Autens in 2005, a consultancy that works closely with schools and local and national authorities to inspire new models of learning, school architecture and learning space design, all in the spirit of user engagement and co-creation. Lene also heads the Global Schools Alliance and serves on several advisory boards.
http://www.autens.dk

Richard Leonard
(Designing for the transition to secondary and beyond)
is an architect and Director of Hayball, one of Australia's largest architecture practices with offices in Melbourne, Sydney and Brisbane. For over 30 years Richard has focused on translating contemporary learning and teaching philosophies into creative design responses. He is a past Chair of the Association for Learning Environments Australasia and a member of the Learning Environments Applied Research Network (LEaRN) at the University of Melbourne, where he participates in several education research initiatives.
www.hayball.com.au

Andy Piggott
(Science laboratories and preparation rooms)
is a retired science education consultant. Andy specialized in advising schools, organizations and the Department for Education on school science accommodation in the UK. He created and led the Lab Design course at the National Science Learning Centre, York, and was project officer for the Laboratory Design for Teaching and Learning project. He is also the author of four School Science Architecture Special Reports and two national reports on the state of school laboratories.

Diane Pumphrey
(How to engage learners)
is the principal of West Thornton Primary Academy. She has been a teacher at West Thornton for 26 years and principal for the last four. Born and raised in the local area, she has spent her career committed to providing children with skills and opportunities that will even the playing field for life after school. Her focus of many years at West Thornton has been to develop children's independence and agency over their own learning.
http://thesynaptictrust.org/our-schools/west-thornton-primary-academy

Kerri Ranney
(AIA, REFP)
is a thought-leader in educational planning and design. As Vice President of Educational Practice at Huckabee, she helps public school districts shape progressive learning environments around culture and curriculum. Kerri also leads research efforts at Huckabee's Learning Experience Laboratories, a unique collaborative focused on the impact of educational design on student engagement at the elementary grades.
www.huckabee-inc.com

Sir Ken Robinson
(Foreword)
works with governments, education systems, international agencies, global corporations and some of the world's leading cultural organizations to unlock the creative energy of people and organizations. The embodiment of the prestigious TED Conference and its commitment to spreading new ideas, Sir Ken Robinson is the most-watched speaker in TED's history. His 2006 talk, 'Do Schools Kill Creativity?' has been viewed over 40 million times by an estimated 350 million people in 160 countries. His latest book, *Creative Schools: The Grassroots Revolution That's Transforming Education* (Viking, 2015), tackles the critical issue of how to transform the world's troubled educational systems and is now available in 15 languages.
http://sirkenrobinson.com

Gary Spracklen
(Technology and communications)
is the headteacher at The Prince of Wales School in Dorchester, a former Digital Educator of the Year and a member of the UK government's Department for Education's 'ETAG' (Educational Technology Action Group). Gary holds the 'Educational Technology Director' Chair for A4LE UK and Europe.
www.princeofwales.dorset.sch.uk

Dave Strudwick
(How can space provoke learning?)
is the headteacher at Plymouth School of Creative Arts, where he has been involved in its design and development from prior to opening. The school is an all-through school for ages from three to sixteen, which uses a project-based, community approach to contextualize and enhance learning. His passion for learning, space, leadership and developing others has been built through a variety of experiences and roles. This includes working with excluded children, co-creating the project that resulted in nine and ten year-olds becoming peer-reviewed published scientists, working with athletes around the development of a coaching culture in schools, and leading and developing a number of successful schools. His interest in technology to enable the transformation of learning is based on a curiosity of what might be possible.
https://plymouthschoolofcreativearts.co.uk

Joe Jack Williams
(Post-occupancy evaluation)
is an engineer, and following a career as a building services consultant he moved on to study for an EngD at The Bartlett Faculty of the Built Environment, University College London (UCL), with support from Feilden Clegg Bradley Studios. Joe's EngD focused on the influence of the school building, with a high-level study examining the performance of the BSF programme, and a detailed holistic study of four schools measuring perceptions, environmental performance and building forms. Joe currently works as a researcher within Feilden Clegg Bradley Studios, developing and enabling research across the practice, and as an associate lecturer within Oxford Brookes, teaching environmental design to architecture students.
https://fcbstudios.com

PICTURE CREDITS

Opposite
An organized science prep room will help technicians prepare experiments